RESCUING BIODIVERSITY

RESCUING BIODIVERSITY

The Protection and Restoration of a North Louisiana Ecosystem

JOHNNY ARMSTRONG

foreword by Kelby Ouchley

Louisiana State University Press
Baton Rouge

Published by Louisiana State University Press
lsupress.org

LSU Press Paperback Original

Manufactured in the United States of America
First printing

Designer: Barbara Neely Bourgoyne
Typeface: Adobe Text Pro
Printer and binder: Versa Press

All photographs courtesy of the author unless otherwise noted.
Jacket photograph courtesy of the author.

Library of Congress Cataloging-in-Publication Data
Names: Armstrong, Johnny, author. | Ouchley, Kelby, 1951– writer
    of foreword.
Title: Rescuing biodiversity : the protection and restoration of a North
    Louisiana ecosystem / Johnny Armstrong ; foreword by Kelby Ouchley.
Description: Baton Rouge : Louisiana State University Press, [2023] |
    Includes bibliographical references and index.
Identifiers: LCCN 2022049604 | ISBN 9780807179505 (paperback)
    restoration—Louisiana. | Upland ecology—Louisiana.
Classification: LCC QH76.5.L8 A76 2023 | DDC
    577.509763/91—dc23/eng/20221116

LC record available at https://lccn.loc.gov/2022049604

for Karen, Cody, Abby, Eva,
Tullie, Bain, Opal, and Clara Eileen

Contents

Foreword

Biodiversity: all the variety of life forms in a certain area, commonly considered at the scale of ecosystems. Is it even possible to comprehend the vastness of this definition? Scientists recently estimated the number of species on Earth at one 1 trillion, with only a tiny fraction of one percent of these being described. The enormity of life assures that we don't know what we don't know about such matters in spite of our best efforts to mine the potential knowledge for three hundred years. What is beginning to surface, though, in addition to new species, is a multitude of previously unknown and remarkable connections among life forms—connections that are critical to the well-being of otherwise unrelated organisms. More than ever before, humans are seen to be dependent on the workings of other species that we barely understand.

There is another element of biodiversity that is more obvious, at least as it pertains to macro-organisms, or those that we can see: the indisputable fact that many are in alarming decline. Extinction rates are rising at a rate never before noted in the history of our species. And for those who objectively consider the scientific facts, the root cause of the global losses at both the population and species level is clearly the behavior of *Homo sapiens*. What is unclear is how long it will take for humans to seriously address the existential threats. There are reasons to be hopeful. Calls for international cooperation to address the problems are gaining traction. Action plans are being developed, and the consensus is that governments alone can't fix our dilemma. The assiduous behavior of individuals is essential.

Rescuing Biodiversity relates the story of one person's efforts to make a difference in the conservation of biodiversity at a scale that he can impact. A pathologist by trade, Johnny Armstrong recognized that worsening problems exist, apprenticed himself to experts in the field, and set out to change things for the better on his property in North Louisiana.

Armstrong presents the facts regarding the loss of global biodiversity and argues that it is worth saving for more than aesthetic reasons. He focuses on Wafer Creek Ranch, his property in the Gulf Coastal Plain ecoregion, and specifically on the remnant flora of shortleaf pine-oak-hickory woodlands. Starting with an anthropogenic, botanical mess, he undertakes a journey to restore the historic ecotype of the area. He addresses dozens of species of relevant plants with text and photos worthy of a field guide. He relates the vital connections between them and other life forms. Discussing challenges, restoration techniques, and critical partners, he charts his path to "rescue biodiversity" as an example for all to follow, regardless of whether your landscape is a patch of bare ground adjacent a to sidewalk or 10,000 acres of former prairie. His enthusiasm alone is inspirational. His mission (and many similar ones that everyone should endorse) is critical.

—KELBY OUCHLEY

Acknowledgments

My work in the restoration and protection of my home's ecosystems has been a long and interesting journey. However, I must say that throughout my course of endeavor, I could not have gotten far without the help of experts. In fact, I couldn't have gotten anywhere. Here, I want to recognize a few of those individuals who have served as my guides, mentors, and ecosystem protectors along my path of learning. First, and continuing to this day, is the mentorship, expertise, and guidance from my dear friend and brother in the cause, Latimore Smith. Latimore is a field botanist and restoration ecologist recently retired from The Nature Conservancy and now, with Nelwyn McInnis, a founding partner in the company Southern Wild Heritage, a consulting service giving advice and expertise for the benefit of those like me who want to take up the challenge of rescuing biodiversity on their own lands. Nelwyn, Latimore's wife and a retired Nature Conservancy biologist, is also land steward for the Land Trust for Louisiana, a wonderful organization that offers permanent protection of vital habitats on private lands for landowners who wish to leave behind a living legacy when they're gone. Nelwyn is my "little sister in the cause."

Dr. Chris Reid, instructor of botany, Louisiana State University–Baton Rouge, has for years been an extremely valuable resource for me in the identification of plant species, many of which appear in this work.

How lucky I was when, early one fall, Chris brought Dr. Lowell Urbatsch, Louisiana State University botany professor and expert on the sunflower family, to Wafer Creek Ranch to help us identify grassland species. It was then that I gained brand-new respect for the goldenrods of Wafer Creek Ranch.

I must acknowledge The Nature Conservancy of Louisiana for taking under its wing four hundred acres of Wafer Creek Ranch to be held and protected in perpetuity within its conservation easement. Without permanent protection, the vital biodiversity of Wafer Creek Ranch would inevitably be destroyed in the future. It was two of my friends, Richard Martin and Dan Weber, both staff biologists with The Nature Conservancy, who fought unceasingly to see that the protection would finally come to pass.

I owe a heavy debt of gratitude to two individuals who are experts in the intricate legalities of the oil and gas industry and its interface with private landowners, including their familiarity with the specific companies that have legal interests in the subsurface minerals pertaining to Wafer Creek Ranch. Logan Hunt, oil and gas advisor with Argent Financial Group, and Matt May, oil and gas attorney, worked tirelessly in their effort to see that the ecosystems of Wafer Creek Ranch would be protected in perpetuity so that the conservation easement, required for that protection, could be completed.

My many thanks to Kelby Ouchley, biologist, former manager of national wildlife refuges, novelist, and well-known author of essays and books on the biodiversity of our state, for writing the foreword for this work. The same thanks go to the manuscript's expert beta readers: Latimore Smith, Nelwyn McInnis, Will deGravelles (ecologist for The Nature Conservancy of Louisiana), Chris Reid, Chris Doffitt (botanist, Louisiana Department of Wildlife and Fisheries), and Larry Allain (emeritus botanist, US Geological Survey Wetland and Aquatic Research Center). All these scientists are botanists and/or restoration ecologists intimately familiar with the grassland communities of the South. I am truly grateful for all their efforts to keep me honest.

Thanks to Lois Deveneau for her indispensable role in the editing and formatting of this work, and for patiently taking up my slack due to my lack of knowledge in "all those electronical things." I really can't imagine any possible way I could have completed the project without her. I am also grateful to Christine Pietryla Wetzler for her editing and promotion.

Thank you, Jenny Keegan, Neal Novak, Todd Manza, Sunny Rosen, and James Wilson, my editors and promoters with Louisiana State University Press, for your kindness, encouragement, and help throughout this process.

Finally, my thanks to Bryan Daniels for his work in the native grass and wildflower seeding on Wafer Creek Ranch, a task that my aging back no longer permits me to do.

Last but certainly not least, I want to express my deepest appreciation to my family for their continued support, so necessary in enabling me to carry out this project.

RESCUING BIODIVERSITY

Introduction

Rescuing Biodiversity: The Protection and Restoration of a North Louisiana Ecosystem is not my book only. Several good people have poured their own time, attention, and expertise into it, along with their suggestions for making it better, and corrections when I went astray. These expert beta readers never asked for payment. I've done my best in my effort to pull it all together into readable story form. And all the while, Grandmother Earth is hurting. This book is an opportunity to help her. All author proceeds must go to conservation of the remaining biodiversity in our state in the form of donation to such organizations as the Land Trust for Louisiana, The Nature Conservancy of Louisiana, and others.

How fortunate I am to have lived for forty-one years on Wafer Creek Ranch (WCR), a native old-growth forest and woodland that stands just outside my front and back doors, always waiting for my exploration to teach me the lessons to be gained by visual observation, by listening, by tasting, by smelling, and by touching its boundless gifts of flora and fauna.

And how honored I am that Wafer Creek Ranch has become a living laboratory utilized by professors and students at Louisiana Tech University for research and learning. For many years I have held the belief that they are the teachers who have the most sway in our lives. That Wafer Creek Ranch has become an important part of that process is another dream come true.

I want to make it clear that I am not an expert naturalist or a formally trained field scientist. So please understand that I do see the precarious nature of this undertaking. I like to think that my approach has been a little bit like that of a science journalist. I hope that's true.

So, here I am. And it's in large part because I am a grandfather who is extremely worried about what we are doing to the biosphere of our planet and how it's going to affect the future of my grandchildren and everybody else's grandchildren and all the generations to follow. If one says I present a doom-and-gloom viewpoint at the beginning of this work, then my answer is this: if a diseased patient is to be healed, first the disease must be diagnosed and its behavior and prognosis understood before proper treatment can be instituted. I don't know of any diseases that are particularly pleasant—if anybody does, I'd like to hear about it.

The biosphere of planet Earth has obviously become unhealthy; it's as if it has contracted a serious disease and is in need of immediate intensive care. We must understand that's the situation we presently face and why it exists, so that we can address this problem. As world-renowned biologist Edward O. Wilson put it, "We are playing a global endgame."[1]

It's my intent with this story to begin by briefly, but factually, telling it like it is regarding the crisis of global biodiversity destruction—the disease we face and what it means—and how ecosystem restoration of the shortleaf pine-oak-hickory woodland can serve as a single example of the many effective treatment modalities we need to bring to bear—not next year—but *right now.* My labor in ecosystem protection and restoration is merely a tiny step, but tiny steps can add up when like-minded concerned people begin, through their own actions, to become soldiers in the cause.

I have only one qualification pertaining to this work: I am a student. And like so many citizens, I have the history of a long lifetime of intense love for nature. As well, I have nearly a decade and a half of on-the-job experience in restoration ecology under the guidance of the best of scientific knowledge in this field that The Nature Conservancy can offer—and The Nature Conservancy is, in my opinion, one of the foremost leaders in the science. I have been lucky to have a close association and friendship with some of the finest field scientists in Louisiana, including those in field botany and restoration ecology.

As a journalistic work, *Rescuing Biodiversity* is intended for the general public interested in nature and our present-day dire conservation issues, for my fellow landowners who might wish to gain protection (with or without restoration) for their own lands and the natural habitats they may harbor, for conservation scientists and students, and especially for my family, who will someday inherit the property—a property that serves in this work as a reasonable example of the protection and restoration of a forest, a woodland, and a grassland ecosystem.

After I address some of the reasons why we need to rescue biodiversity, both from the global perspective and that of the Upper West Gulf Coastal Plain, I will begin a description of the Wafer Creek Ranch restoration, starting with a brief outline of the ecology of its historic woodland overstory and its groundcover. In discussing the groundcover, I will examine a few of its salient grasses and wildflowers. With the forb and shrub wildflowers, I have, because of their vital support of biodiversity, dwelled more heavily on the families of legumes (peas) and composites (sunflowers), but I have added a few more based on personal preference and the necessary roles they play within their grassland environment, such as the milkweeds, spurges, passion flowers, mints, and others. Where I was able, I have tried to add in examples of the connections and interactions of these plant species with other plants, the soil, and the animal species that live within their environment.

Later, I describe in some detail my work in the restoration, how it began, the major plant communities of Wafer Creek Ranch, and finally, the results of the restoration work so far, which will consist largely of a field trip of pictures and captions.

The appendixes offer a short list of ways people can get back to nature in our state and a working list of the grassland plants of Wafer Creek Ranch. Within the book I took more liberty by including a few plant species not necessarily associated with a grassland community.

There has been significant progress in restoration of the longleaf pine woodlands and savannas of the coastal areas of Louisiana and adjoining coastal states, of which The Nature Conservancy, the Longleaf Alliance, and federal and state agencies have played a particularly successful role that is ongoing. In fact, E. O. Wilson declared these coastal grassland ecosystems "one of the richest ground floras in North America."[2]

There also is an abundance of grassland biodiversity that can be reawakened in the uplands of North Louisiana and adjoining states, but so far, attempts at this vital work have been somewhat paltry. I hope this book not only can provide a brief overview of the serious problems our future generations must face in surviving a diminishing biosphere but also serve as an example, on the local level, of what restoration of the North Louisiana hill country woodlands can give back to nature and our grandchildren's future. After all, there really *is* gold in them there hills.

I

Why Does Our Planet's Biosphere Need to Be Rescued?

Several years ago, a small group of Louisiana Tech University students was assisting ornithologist Dr. Terri Maness in the mist-netting and banding of birds on Wafer Creek Ranch. I said a few words to the group about the restoration on Wafer Creek Ranch, and one of the students, Dan, asked why I would go to the trouble of taking on such an onerous project instead of simply leaving the human-altered forest alone. Dan's question was simple, yet to me profound. I hope this work will provide an adequate case for why both protection and restoration are so vital for the future, as far as how we are going to address the crisis of our vanishing biodiversity.

There could be several answers to Dan's question, but one answer could be that bringing an ecosystem back to close to what it was in precolonial times would create something on the order of a museum piece to show us what it looked like back in the days when the only people around were Native. What did they see and what did they know when they hunted and gathered in those times long past, and how did their connection to their natural surroundings affect their very survival and their culture? That's not a bad answer, in my opinion. But there's an *even better, far better, reason that will unfold as we move deeper into the story.*

When astronauts on the International Space Station look down on our planet from space, they often are struck by an entirely new perspective on their global home—its beauty and the absence of any recognizable national borders. Above all, they perceive its fragility. They see a thin blue layer of atmosphere on Earth's horizon hovering over an exquisitely thin layer of life's habitable zone below. That thin layer is where Earth's biosphere exists—all of it—except for the astronaut observers themselves on the ISS. As a result of this new perspective, many of them see themselves differently. This reaction is called the overview effect, a term coined by Frank White in his 1987 book of the same name, and it often leaves these scientists with the sense that they no longer identify with any nationality, race, or culture. Rather, they identify only as citizens of planet Earth.[1]

It seems as if the overview effect might be a form of intellectual maturity—the revelation that occurs in the mind of someone who has awakened with a clearer insight into reality.

As we enter the time of radical negative impact from the effects of human-caused climate change, we must clearly recognize an additional looming threat just as ominous. The ever-increasing rate of global destruction of species and ecosystems is a grave threat on a planetary scale. As astronauts have recognized, our planet's thin zone where life exists is fragile and should be treated as such.

I have to wonder whether our species might need a grand dose of the overview effect to wake it up to the fact that it is headed down the road to catastrophe—one unlike any that modern humans have seen before in our roughly 200,000-year history. Would it not be better to meet this problem as a species that sees itself as citizens of Earth, that recognizes we are all connected to one another and to the biosphere from which we came?

The seriousness of the problem we face has been well addressed by the late world-renowned biologist and two-time Pulitzer Prize winner, E. O. Wilson: "The on-going mass extinction of species, and with it, the extinction of genes and ecosystems, ranks with pandemics, world war and climate change as among the deadliest threats that humanity has imposed on itself."[2]

Wilson's quote certainly addresses the gravity of the problem, and the following is only a partial list of the evidence, or signs and symptoms, of the malady we face.

AMPHIBIANS

A 2016 report from the US Geological Survey informs us that amphibians in the United States are facing an annual decline of nearly 4 percent, and according to the International Union for Conservation of Nature, more than 40 percent of amphibians are imperiled and threatened with extinction. The causes include pollution, wetland loss, disease (such as the fungal disease chytridiomycosis), and invasive nonnative species.[3]

BUTTERFLIES

According to numerous sources, butterflies are in broad decline, with several known extinctions in the recent past. Twenty-four species of butterfly are presently listed as endangered by the US Fish and Wildlife Service. Losses are mainly attributed to habitat destruction, pesticides, and climate change.[4]

BEES

There are about 4,000 native bee species in North America and fifty of those are bumblebee species. Bumblebees are one of the most efficient pollinating insect groups. But bumblebees are in peril and declining, and causes include habitat loss, climate change, disease, and pesticides, particularly the neon-icotinoid insecticides.[5]

BIRDS

The National Audubon Society states that 389 of the 604 regularly occurring bird species in North America (north of Mexico) are vulnerable to extinction. Audubon scientists say that within eighty years bird field guides could become half the size that they presently are. And a recent finding by the Cornell Lab of Ornithology, in collaboration with other universities, has determined that since 1970 the total bird population in North America (north of Mexico) has declined by 30 percent, a loss in total bird numbers of 3 billion since 1970—all largely due to habitat loss, global warming, and other human causes. A reasonable analogy might be the dead canary in the coal mine. The scientists say the time to act is right now.[6]

Based on my personal birding experience of forty years, I can well believe that there are 3 billion fewer birds than was the case in the early 1970s. For years, my wife, Karen, and I have been watching this day, once long in the future, unfold before our eyes. We are today haunted by all those little ghosts of the past, of backyard migrant species once common but now become unusual sightings. Karen and I remember the days when we would come to a stop on our driveway and wait for a momma bobwhite and her babies to cross. Now, sadly, I haven't heard a bobwhite calling on Wafer Creek Ranch since about fourteen years ago. Roadrunners, loggerhead shrikes, and eastern meadowlarks have become unusual sightings. What happened to the hundreds of grackles that would cover our yards in winter? And the list goes on.

FRESHWATER FISH

Over the latter part of the nineteenth and into the twenty-first century, 57 freshwater fish species in North America went extinct due to human activity—causes include habitat-destructive damming of rivers and streams, spring-head filling and destruction, pollution, introduction of invasive species, and draining of natural ponds and lakes. According to the American Fisheries Society, 40 percent of freshwater fish species in North America are imperiled or already extinct.[7]

OCEAN SPECIES

Three billion people, nearly half of the world's population, depend on fish as a protein source. Yet around 85 percent of commercially harvested marine fishing stocks are at their breaking point due to overharvesting.[8]

According to a report from the Union of Concerned Scientists, one example of the contribution of pollution to the growing problem of the loss of sustainability of ocean ecosystems is terrestrial runoff of nitrogenous fertilizer compounds from farms of the Midwestern United States. Those compounds wind up in the Mississippi River, travel downstream, and empty into the Gulf of Mexico, both from the Mississippi and from its distributary, the Atchafalaya River. This nitrogen runoff creates a large low-oxygen-level "dead zone" that can no longer support the viability of fish and shrimp, thus causing massive losses to the fish and shrimp industry.[9]

Coral reef ecosystems are imperiled and declining due to warming ocean temperature and ocean acidification. The acidification, a rather complicated story of seawater chemistry beyond the scope of this text, is ultimately caused by absorption of increased atmospheric CO_2, largely due to human activity (mainly the burning of fossil fuels).

MUSSELS

Of the 302 known species of mussel in North America, 26 are extinct and another 87 species are federally listed as endangered or threatened. The cause is primarily water pollution.[10] Up to 70 percent, however, are at least imperiled, because of water pollution, disease, and damming of streams and rivers.

FOREST WILDLIFE

In 2019, the World Wildlife Fund released its *Below the Canopy* report, a global assessment of forest biodiversity. The report revealed that monitored populations of forest-dwelling wildlife species have declined on average by more than half since 1970. The hardest hit were tropical species. For instance, Greenpeace has reported that over a sixteen-year period, half of the orangutans of Borneo have been wiped out due to forest destruction. Furthermore, their analysis shows that Indonesian rainforest deforestation increased by 50 percent during the COVID-19 pandemic, "all due to the constant attack by the agribusiness industry and governments preferring corporate interests over protecting people and ecosystems . . . All over the world," they say, "we are seeing governments eliminate environmental regulations and relax enforcement to fast-track exploitative development."[11]

MAMMALS

According to the International Union for Conservation of Nature, one-fourth of all mammals are threatened with extinction—no wonder, when we see today's report card on the Borneo orangutans and when we follow the desperate situation of North American hibernating bats infected by the fungus that causes white-nose syndrome. The latter has caused the crash of several North American bat species and is due to human introduction of a European fungal pathogen. This was no doubt accidental, yet the effect is the same.[12]

PLANTS

Plant diversity is also in rapid global decline, a direct result of habitat destruction and global warming. Perhaps a third of all land plants are at risk of extinction, including many that are undescribed or are described but otherwise data deficient.[13] From 1996 to 2015, more than 28 million acres of Canada's boreal forests were logged out, largely to make "extra-soft" toilet paper. A 2019 United Nations report estimates that 24 billion metric tons of fertile soil are lost each year, and according to a 2015 article in *Nature,* 15 billion trees are cut down each year.[14]

The effect of climate change on plants is a complicated subject that deserves at least a brief, though necessarily partial, explanation. Generally, with a warming planet, plants become subjected to increased heat stress, which causes an increase in water needs. With expected prolonged droughts, the stress on plants is further aggravated and may become lethal. Additionally, higher atmospheric CO_2 levels promote plant growth, particularly invasive species that crowd out native grasses and wildflowers. Finally, due to global warming, native plants bloom earlier and may become asynchronous with the appearance of pollinators. Thus, the insect pollinators lose part of their vital pollen and nectar source and native plant species lose their means of pollination.[15] There are other important causes of native plant decline in a warming world, such as saltwater intrusion from rising sea levels and devastating wildfires.

The facts I've just outlined represent only a fraction of our global threat, and much of it represents North America or the United States alone. However, it is significant for us to realize that with biodiversity, as it is with real estate, location means everything. Only 5 percent of Earth's land surface encompasses tropical rainforest zones. Yet tropical rainforests are the home to more (perhaps far more) than 50 percent of the entire biodiversity of planet Earth. Tragically, the tropical rainforests are being systematically destroyed, permanently extinguishing untold numbers of species of animals and plants before ever being identified by humans. In many ways, it seems that the better the economy and technology, the faster the destruction. Everywhere. Not just in rainforests.[16]

According to the World Wildlife Fund's *Living Planet Report 2016,* "Global wildlife populations fell by 58 percent between 1970 and 2012 and will likely shrink to one-third of their 1970 numbers by 2020." Nik Sekhran of the United Nations Development Program further says, "We've entered a mass extinction event—only the sixth in Earth's history. Our planet may now be losing species faster than during the Chicxulub asteroid strike that wiped out the dinosaurs 66 million years ago. This time, however, the culprit is us."[17]

This statement comes from the National Geographic Society in 2019: "Earth is currently experiencing a biodiversity crisis. Recent estimates suggest that extinction threatens up to a million species of plants and animals, in large part because of human activities."[18]

According to the United Nations Environment Programme, "Earth is in the midst of a mass extinction of life. Scientists estimate that 150–200 species of plant, insect, bird and mammal become extinct every twenty-four hours."[19]

Even if the most conservative estimate of global loss of species is correct, at 150 per day, in twenty years, the loss would amount to more than 1 million species. Just two decades. So now we begin to really see how the comparison with the Chicxulub asteroid strike that wiped out the dinosaurs at the end of the Cretaceous starts to make sense.

In his book, *Half-Earth,* E. O. Wilson references a convenient acronym for the causes of biodiversity destruction. With the letters occurring in decreasing rank of magnitude, it is HIPPO:

H = habitat destruction and climate change
I = invasive nonnative species
P = pollution
P = population of *Homo sapiens*
O = overharvesting

Addressing these five issues is, to say the least, a monumental task. It's doable, but only if we all come together to meet the monster head-on, which might take the will of most of the people of Earth, particularly its leaders. But the alternative is unthinkable. There is no paradise planet out there waiting for us to colonize it when we've ruined the biosphere of our own. There are no giant alien rescue ships that will come a'ridin' down to save us. The high likelihood of life on other planets, exoplanets, and moons notwithstanding, we are alone. Alone with our kin, the plant and animal species along whose sides we have evolved through the process of natural selection for around 3.8 billion years, whose genes we share in our own DNA. What foolish arrogance would oversee their destruction?

Humans do not have "dominion" over Earth. Such a concept of humanity's relationship with Earth's biodiversity is full of arrogance and false identity. Mother Nature isn't always sweet, but she is always in charge. And the sooner we realize it, the better.

In my novel *Shadowshine: An Animal Adventure* (Guernica World Editions, 2019), the animal characters of the story, called the forest-folk, have a message for their readers: humanity has an identity crisis in the face of nature. Humans don't know what they are.[20]

How can we know what we are if we don't understand, in a down-deep and meaningful way, that we are a part of nature, that we are merely animals that exist in Earth's biosphere along with our genetic kin within the family of life—*all* life, including animals, plants, microbes, and so on—with whom our ancestors of the deep past lived and evolved since the beginning of life on Earth?

Our lack of self-identity allows us to become disconnected from the natural world, and in doing so, we relegate nature (Earth's biodiversity) to something separate and at a "lower" level than ourselves. This is dangerous because it turns nature into something remote and expendable, and consequently, easy to exploit and destroy. That is exactly what is happening today: the global destruction of species and ecosystems at an ever-increasing rate.

The forest-folk recognized that they, along with every single organism now living and those locked away far in the past, are indeed the kin of humans. This should not be a very difficult concept to grasp. In fact, it's old science of evolutionary biology as well as old custom among Native peoples going back centuries, if not millennia. So, we might ask ourselves, why shouldn't we all embrace the nature–human connectedness and kinship so well expressed and celebrated by the Native peoples of what we now call North America? After all, they seem to get it.

Several years ago, Karen and I attended the Calgary Stampede in Alberta, Canada, where we went straight to the First Nations section. There, we saw the inspiring traditional (prairie) chicken dance of the Blackfoot people. I stood with my hand over my mouth and watched these athletic First Nations performers in their traditional dress crouched low, weaving to the drumbeat the mating dance of a bird of the prairie that they knew and deeply respected. It was emotional. And it came to me that I was witnessing members of my own species who just maybe, after all, know what they are.

Although it seems the forest-folk are correct in pointing out humanity's identity crisis as a cause of our destruction of Earth's family of life, to which humanity itself belongs, it cannot be the only reason. There may be many. It seems obvious that tribalism, a cause of our aggressive behavior, and greed are surely contributors also. There is reasonable scientific evidence that these two traits are hardwired into our genome.[21] How do we control our own genetically hardwired traits? We are not there yet, but if we were, would we change our own genome?

Does our species even have a truly stand-alone high intellectual capacity in the first place? Would such a species develop an advanced technology and then turn around and use it to destroy its own home planet as well as itself? Are we simply not properly forged by our own evolutionary biology to control ourselves?

Cosmologists have for years contemplated the question of whether technologically advanced alien species on other worlds are the common thing. In his world-famous book *Cosmos,* Carl Sagan, in his discussion of the likelihood of technologically advanced alien civilizations in our galaxy, said, "Perhaps civilizations arise repeatedly, inexorably, on innumerable planets in the Milky Way, but are generally unstable; so all but a tiny fraction are unable to survive their technology and succumb to greed and ignorance, pollution and nuclear war." Sagan also spoke of the hypothetical receipt of a message from space as it being a "profoundly hopeful sign. It means that someone has learned to live with high technology; that it is possible to survive technological adolescence."[22]

Ironically, because of today's information and communications technology, we can now witness ourselves, in almost real-time, madly rushing to dismantle the biosphere on which we depend. At least we can hope that our bearing witness to this destructive adolescent behavior will allow us to ascend the learning curve to the point where we begin listening to the advice of our dedicated scientists. Perhaps that will be humanity's overview effect. We can only hope.

Presently, for the first time in Earth's 4.5 billion–year history, our planet may be faced with a global mass extinction event caused by a single species. Will *Homo sapiens* be among the missing in the near future?

E. O. Wilson believed that it has taken around 10 million years for planet Earth to get back up to speed with its evolutionary biology and species diversity after each of its five mass-extinction events in the past. That's really not that long, considering the long life of Earth's biological engine. We, at least, can take some comfort in knowing that if our species cannot control itself enough to prevent a mass extinction event and its own demise in the process, at least planet Earth and its amazing family of life will rehabilitate itself and live on without us.

Being aware of our genomic background as it relates to our behavior is important information for us to have as we go forward. Yet we can never use it as an excuse for destructive behavior. Our intellectual ability to cooperatively meet the challenges ahead in order to improve the lives and welfare of our future generations seem also embedded in our genetic tool kit. In her interviews with scientists at the Max Planck Institute for Evolutionary Anthropology, author Elizabeth Kolbert came away with this impression: "In general, apes seem to lack the impulse toward collective problem solving that's so central to human society."[23] We simply must realize that we, as a species, in spite of whatever genomic disadvantages we have, do have what it takes to meet our biggest challenge ever. And we might wish to recall that our very presence tells us that we, like the monarch butterfly, have what it takes to run the gauntlet of 3.8 billion years of natural selection.

Why Should We Worry About "Little Species"?

Some people may ask, "Why should we really care about, say, a monarch butterfly? After all, it is only an insect." But if you ever have the opportunity to see a monarch butterfly or any other species in peril (and these days there's no shortage), the answer would be right before your eyes.

For one thing, we humans are the reason the monarch is in peril. We are the cause of the destruction of its habitat, in both its winter and its summer zones. The eastern population depends on the very restricted zones of oyamel fir forests in the central Mexican highlands in winter, and access to native milkweed in North America during spring and summer. The eastern monarchs are totally dependent on both for their survival. But the oyamel forests are being destroyed by illegal logging and native milkweed in North America is being destroyed by habitat destruction, global warming, pesticides, and other factors.

Is this okay? Perhaps morality ultimately comes down to a personal question, but there's a large, if not growing, segment of our population that thinks it's indeed immoral to blatantly and knowingly cause the loss of a species that has survived the evolutionary gauntlet only to now find itself the neighbor of humans in today's world. We, their human neighbors, have the power to crush this butterfly species. So, do we simply tell it (ourselves, actually), "We recognize you as a lovely little creature with an amazing life story, but in the final analysis and with heavy hearts we must inform you that we simply cannot find you a place in our business model of the future."

Again, the doubters might say we should accept collateral damage, and it's costly to rescue imperiled little animals and plants.

But what money value does one really place on a species? Should monetary value apply in such a case? It's a fact that insect populations are in serious decline, largely for the same reasons that the monarch is: ecosystem destruction, global warming, pesticides, and other factors, such as disease and invasive nonnative species, all of which *we* cause. Bird, bat, freshwater fish, reptile, and amphibian species are almost totally dependent on insects as a food source for their survival. Should we let them go too? What's the monetary value for that? Are we as a species willing to give up the important ecosystem service of insect pollination, which we depend on for a sizable portion of our own food supply?

If an animal group can be said to have dominion over Earth, it seems reasonable that it might be the insects. It's estimated that 90 percent of the animal species on Earth are insects. About 1 million species of insects have been classified so far, and presently entomologists believe that this number is less than 10 percent of those still uncounted.

Insects first appeared about 480 million years ago, during the Ordovician period, and flying insects showed up in the Devonian, about 400 million years ago, when terrestrial plants were beginning to thrive. During the Carboniferous, more than 300 million years ago, insects grew large; the wingspans of some dragonflies were more than two feet, due to an atmosphere that was highly saturated with oxygen. It's easy to reason that the biosphere of Earth is well accustomed to having insects around as its principal citizens and that it's highly dependent on them as a major pillar of its infrastructure.

But we now have an ominous situation that is only recently coming into focus—the massive decline of insect populations. Over a period from 1989 to 2016—twenty-seven years—entomologists covering sixty-three protected sites in Germany documented an average decrease in flying insect biomass of 75 percent.[1] And similar insect disappearances are being documented around the globe, including in the United States.

There is no way to overstate how critical insects are for the maintenance of ecosystems. Not only are insects vital in the food chain but also about 75 percent of flowering plants depend on insect pollination. Additionally, insects are dispersers of seeds, and they are vital decomposers, reducing carcasses, dead wood, and dung into usable nutrients for the soil.

E. O. Wilson is quoted as saying that if humans suddenly disappeared, Earth would "regenerate back to the rich state of equilibrium that existed 10,000 years ago. If insects were to vanish, the environment would collapse into chaos."[2]

We humans are left with absolutely no excuse for inaction.

FIG. 1. Monarch butterfly

It's not too late to mitigate the evolving disaster. The movement to combat global warming is growing worldwide and someday soon will reach the level of priority it has for too long deserved. And combating global warming will be good for combating global destruction of species and ecosystems, primarily because global warming severely impacts ecosystems. The reverse is also true. Protecting and restoring native forests, wetlands, peatlands, seagrass, and terrestrial grassland ecosystems, and thus the carbon capture provided by these systems, is of major importance in the slowing and eventual stopping of global warming.

We the public must not be reticent or shy about standing up for what is needed to rescue biodiversity and combat global warming. We should use our voices in as many forms as possible. In order to face this problem together, wouldn't be best if the support of effective policies to address global warming and the global crisis of species and ecosystem loss becomes a litmus test in our voting decisions? After all, isn't it our duty to do whatever we can to leave a sustainable future for the generations that come after us?

In my hometown of Ruston, Louisiana, we celebrate Earth Day, and we get a fair event turnout, especially because it's a college town. I think it's more important than we might realize that we make a showing at such events (especially with our families!) as well as attending any peaceful marches or protests on behalf of the environment and combating global warming. In this way we can show our children and grandchildren that we're with them and we are into the cause—that we are concerned for their future.

Another easy way to support this important cause of rescuing biodiversity is to keep abreast of the many excellent environmental groups available to us. They need our support, and we need their work, which might include on-the-ground protection and restoration of ecosystems to fighting court battles on behalf of environmental protections. They also provide valuable information in the literature they distribute to their supporters.

There are signs of hope all around us today as it seems leaders of business are joining the effort. For example, Fred Krupp, president of the Environmental Defense Fund, said, "When the president committed to cutting US greenhouse gas emissions 50 percent below 2005 levels by 2030, he had the public backing of 400 companies and investors, including Apple, Coca-Cola, and Google. And major companies around the world are investing in a groundbreaking initiative to save rainforests."[3]

Another hopeful sign is that leaders of many countries understand the crisis and are demanding action to rescue Earth's declining biosphere. The United Nations Convention on Biological Diversity is constructing a draft agreement designating global protection of 30 percent of land and sea by 2030, and 50 percent by 2050. More than a hundred conservation groups have united under this goal, and the Biden administration is on board.[4] But at this time, much needs to be worked out, such as the crucial stipulation that the newly protected areas are indeed sites of significant biodiversity. Sites of high species richness and endemism must rank as highest priority. And protection must be *real and enforced* protection, not just protection in name only.

But time is not on our side when it comes to this double-barreled threat that so much affects the future of our children and grandchildren and the generations to follow. It's going to take unselfish effort and action on our part to accomplish this feat. We are intellectually capable of doing it. And so we must do it. The alternative is unacceptable.

Here, I'm reminded of the classic movie line so well delivered by Matt Damon in *The Martian*. When his character, Mark Watney, was left behind on Mars, presumed dead, with few rations for survival, no way to contact his crew, and no planned Mars missions within the next four years, Mark said, "In the face of overwhelming odds, I'm left with only one option: I'm gonna have to science the shit out of this."

And so it is with *Homo sapiens* today as we stand at the very edge of the abyss of what may be the sixth great extinction on Earth. This is no time to turn our backs on science. Rather, we must look to science, follow the path that it has carved out and will continue to carve out for us in the future. Only in this way, along with our goodwill to each other and to our fellow living creatures, can we begin to slowly but surely inch backwards from this dreadfully precarious place where we now find ourselves.

What clearer example of the perils of turning our backs on science than that of the more dangerous Delta variant of the COVID–19 virus, which tragically increased human transmission, resulting in more hospitalizations and deaths, all because too many of us refused to follow the science and get vaccinated?

In his discussion of our hominid ancestors' descent from life in the trees to their new Darwinian pathway on the ground, Carl Sagan emphasized the evolutionary advantage of having bigger brains for adapting to the new environment: "Other things being equal, it is better to be smart than stupid."[5]

Let us not allow science denial to be an obstacle as we undertake our mission to leave a living planet to our children. Science will lead us to a better place. But only if we let it.

Many children who are too young to vote, such as the inspiring climate activist Greta Thunberg, see this glaring fact. They are wise enough to call out the politicians bowing to corporate greed for their own personal gain as they turn their backs on science. Children like Greta are not stupid. Quite the contrary. They are clearly aware of the science that is telling them that their world is in trouble and crumbling before their eyes as they watch their elders wither into a helpless state of apathy and excuses while staring into the face of a massive global emergency. As reported by Leanna First-Arai in *Sierra* magazine, students in a Nashville protest sang:

Mama, Mama, can't you hear
The children screaming here and there?
Mama, Mama, can't you see?
This is an emergency.[6]

The children, too, are marking a path for us to follow. We should take heed, for if we deliberately fail them when we could have done more, they will never forget it, and they shouldn't.

Mechanisms of Destruction
and Degradation on the Local Level

The global problem of biodiversity loss is just that—in one way or another, it's everywhere, including right here on the local level, the Upper West Gulf Coastal Plain, which roughly encompasses what we call the Ark-La-Tex region, along with a part of the lands of the Choctaw Nation of southeastern Oklahoma.

All of these mechanisms are typical of what has happened throughout this landscape over the years. So it should be no surprise that the native landscape of Wafer Creek Ranch, where I live, was not spared damage.

AGRICULTURE OF THE PAST

The shortleaf pine-oak-hickory woodland with its intact grassland groundcover is virtually extinct in the Upper West Gulf Coastal Plain ecoregion of our state, and I expect that statement largely holds true throughout the rest of the ecoregion. One of the main reasons goes back to the 1800s, when woodlands and forests were cut down and significant portions of the land were converted to agriculture, mainly cotton farming. The scars from those old days, which extended into the 1940s and 1950s, remain today, as one can still find the old terraces constructed by the Civilian Conservation Corps to prevent soil erosion during the Great Depression and the Dust Bowl years of the 1930s. Also, in the zones where those old, plowed fields once existed, there are no trees today older than about eighty years, and the tree populations that exist are often lacking in the original upland species type.

FIRE SUPPRESSION

Another big reason for the loss of the shortleaf pine-oak-hickory woodland groundcover is a great many years of fire suppression. Periodic fires are a requirement for sustaining a grassland ecosystem, especially in an area of high rainfall such as the southern United States. Without them, the grassland will be lost over time because hot fire is what suppresses the growth of shrub species and fire-sensitive trees that will eventually overtake the grassland and shade it out. Over time the hilltops and upper slopes of Wafer Creek Ranch have indeed been overtaken by the native fire-sensitive tree species that normally resided downslope, where lightning-induced and Native people–ignited fires burned much cooler.

COMMODITY FORESTRY PRACTICES

Over more and more of the countryside, the practice has been to clear-cut standing upland forest, often following with broadcast herbicide, and then to replant the area with stands of pure loblolly pine, a practice that has occurred throughout the Upper West Gulf Coastal Plain ecoregion for many years. The result is not a forest. It is an agricultural crop more akin to a cornfield than to a forest in its ability to support biodiversity. However, cutting loblolly pines and off-site hardwoods (elm, sweetgum, maple, black gum, and the like) and leaving the shortleaf pines and upland hardwoods behind to grow would be truly sustainable and even restorative of the original shortleaf pine-oak-hickory overstory. It's all very well that foresters leave behind strips of trees along riparian zones—obviously that's necessary—but it's simply not enough. Our bottomland forests are also subjected to the damaging practice of clear-cutting. What is the justification for this destructive practice?

It seems that the wood pellets industry thinks it has an answer. Wood pellets are a manufactured product converted from wood, using as its raw material woody debris collected at mills, and trees recently logged out of forests. The pellets are usually shipped overseas to be burned to power electric energy plants, as a way to replace the burning of coal.

This industry is being subsidized by billions of dollars from multiple countries, including European Union member countries and the United States. According to Yale Environment 360, the pellet industry was launched around 2012 after the United Kingdom's Department of Energy and Climate Change developed a policy classifying the burning of woody biomass as a green alternative to transition away from burning coal to generate power. Supposedly, the greenhouse gas emissions from burning the woody biomass would be offset by the carbon capture of regenerating planted forests after logging, or simply letting the forests grow back on their own. This was going to be the great solution to air pollution. And the subsidies soon followed.

The Intergovernmental Panel on Climate Change, not to be confused with the UK's energy policy makers, does not give a green light to burning biomass as an energy source. It states in its latest AR6 report, "large scale deployment of bioenergy, including bioenergy with carbon capture and storage . . . can damage ecosystems directly or through increasing competition for land."

More than 500 scientists signed a letter to President Biden and other world leaders urging them not to substitute burning trees for fossil fuels as a climate solution, writing, "The burning of wood will increase warming for decades to centuries."[1]

At present, there appears to be two major players in this industry: Enviva and Drax, two global giants acting in multiple countries. It seems these two giants have turned their attention to the South, where logging has been ongoing for many decades with little to no regulation.

Enviva's flagship pellet manufacturing plant, located in Ahoskie, North Carolina, gives its residents not only a severe dust pollution problem but also a chance to witness their pristine forested countryside disappear altogether, or perhaps be "reforested" with pine tree monoculture. A study of the Ahoskie plant commissioned by the Southern Environmental Law Center and the National Wildlife Federation found that more than 50 percent of the likely sourcing area for the Ahoskie facility is forested wetlands. More than 168,000 acres of wetland forests are at high risk of being cut down for manufacturing wood pellets at this single plant, the study said.[2]

The European Academies Science Advisory Council (EASAC), basically Europe's counterpart of the US National Academy of Sciences, has recently released its Joint Research Centre's report on the use of woody biomass for energy. The study asks "whether and, if so when, can woody biomass from forests contribute to climate change mitigation." The council says the urgency of the climate crisis requires that any renewable technology must succeed in reducing atmospheric levels of carbon dioxide soon enough to help meet the targets of the Paris Agreement. They further state that with average warming already over 1°C (1.8°F), it appears to EASAC scientists that a "'renewable' energy that actually increases atmospheric CO_2 for decades merely contributes to overshooting the 1.5°C–2°C [2.7°F–3.6°F] targets." They emphasize, "Such technology is not effective in mitigating climate change and even increases the risk of dangerous climate change."

EASAC's JRC report classifies different sources of bioenergy feedstock (what the furnace fire burns to generate electricity) according to the length of time before they "are likely to achieve carbon emission savings compared to fossil fuels into short (1–2 decades), likely medium (3–5 decades), unlikely medium (over 5 decades), and long-term (over a century or never)." The report describes the types of feedstocks that belong to each of these categories.

Christina Moberg, president of EASAC, summarized the results, "The JRC report allows us to assess different sources of biomass from a climate perspective. Unfortunately, this confirms our worst fears that most of the current biomass in coal conversions is in the worst categories. As EASAC has repeatedly pointed out, accounting rules and public subsidies have led to an industry that is reducing even further our chances of meeting Paris Agreement targets."[3]

Word is getting around. Burning biomass as a carbon-neutral alternative to coal doesn't work. According to the Dogwood Alliance, two major financial institutions have down-rated Drax as an unsustainable business model. The global financial institution Citi Group stated, "While sentiment could continue to support what's perceived as a green growth stock . . . we do not fundamentally see biomass as a sustainable source of energy."[4]

Now that Enviva and Drax are moving into Louisiana, they may present themselves as a clean, renewable source of energy. If they do, they are greenwashing.

OIL AND GAS OPERATIONS

Oil and gas exploration has always been destructive. But now the damage is compounded by the practice of exploiting underground oil and gas through fracking, which has become common throughout much of the ecoregion. Its contribution to negative atmospheric changes and global warming notwithstanding, the building of drilling pads for these wells takes up five to ten or more acres of land. The wells are drilled and developed, leaving behind pipelines, roads, and barren areas large enough to maintain the traffic flow of big tanker trucks. The amount of land area destroyed is shocking when one considers the accumulated damage to our ecoregion. Not only is the forest and soil lost, but also the geology is destroyed when large portions of hillsides are removed and draws containing vital hillside seeps and springs are filled to build such large, flat pads.

DEVELOPMENT

"Every 30 seconds, a football field worth of America's natural areas disappears to roads, houses, pipelines, and other development." This shocking quote comes from a 2019 Center for American Progress report.[5] We are all familiar with the damage to ecosystems from urban and suburban development, so-called urban sprawl. Housing, streets, malls, gas stations, stores, and the like, moving farther and farther over the countryside, have caused massive losses to native habitats. Habitat degradation from damage caused by forestry practices, and even by agriculture, can usually be restored (as is the case in some areas on Wafer Creek Ranch), but development results in conversion of native habitats to often irreversible conditions, leaving little to no chance of restoration in the future.

The forestry industry, on which everybody depends in one way or another, is obviously of economic importance in our ecoregion, but maybe it's time for it, as well as the oil and gas industry, to become real partners in mitigation and restoring native forests and woodland communities. We especially need the forest industry to engage in more ecologically sound methods going forward and to mount their efforts at the scale of the problem we are all facing.

The same can be said for landowners (like me) who have the opportunity to save whatever native, biodiverse habitats exist on our lands. After all, 60 percent of the landmass in the United States is privately owned; therefore, it's easy to imagine just how vital landowners are in reaching the science-based 30 percent land protection goal to save these habitats by 2030, and then beyond, to 50 percent by 2050. I truly believe there *has* to be inspiring numbers of private landowners who love their lands and see the need to legally protect whatever native habitats they harbor. Landowners need the opportunity to leave behind a living legacy.

In this regard, land trusts, such as the Land Trust for Louisiana and its national parent organization, the Land Trust Alliance, offer permanent land protection through conservation easement options (which can be quite versatile in fulfilling the needs and wishes of the landowners themselves). Land trusts offer us a real opportunity to become a major force in dragging ourselves back from the abyss. Erin Heskett, vice president for conservation initiatives for the Land Trust Alliance, said, "Voluntary private land conservation is a bipartisan and popular priority, and we're perfectly positioned for 30 x 30 [30 percent of the nation's lands and waters protected by 2030]."[6]

We must also remember there's help through cost sharing from both private and governmental sources, such as the US Department of Agriculture's Natural Resources Conservation Service, state agencies, and in my region, the Lower Mississippi Valley Joint Venture, an organization of both government and nongovernmental organization partners.

We're all in this thing together as we face a monstrous common enemy. And we all know enough about our amazing human ingenuity to realize that we have a seemingly limitless ability to create new and innovative improvements to our present way of doing things.

II

Restoration Ecology of the Shortleaf Pine-Oak-Hickory Woodland

Now we begin a description of the historic woodland-grassland community of the ridges and upper slopes of the hills—the target of the Wafer Creek Ranch restoration. Both topics, the historic woodland plant community and its restoration, are inextricably tied.

It would be impossible for me to discuss this subject, especially with pictures, if not for the progress already made in the Wafer Creek Ranch restoration, demonstrating the overstory and some of the grasses and wildflowers that make up the shortleaf pine-oak-hickory woodland and its grassland groundcover. Fifteen years ago there was no open woodland and hardly any grassland species in sight.

Ecosystem restoration is a vitally needed and growing field of biology. There are various kinds of restoration, depending on the nature and type of ecosystem that existed long before an area became diminished from its historic level of biodiversity. But the only restoration addressed in this work will be that of Wafer Creek Ranch: the shortleaf pine-oak-hickory woodland and its grassland groundcover.

Interestingly, in his masterpiece *The Diversity of Life,* E. O. Wilson said, "Here is the means to end the great extinction spasm. The next century will be the era of restoration in ecology."[1]

That was thirty years ago and still, more than ever, the prediction is profoundly correct. In the face of the ever-increasing global destruction of species and ecosystems, it has become obvious that protection efforts alone are not enough to mitigate the damage. Something more must be done to save our planet's diversity of life. Native ecosystem restoration, in addition to protection, will serve as a critical tool for rescuing Earth's vanishing biodiversity. This is the best answer to the question posed by Louisiana Tech student, Dan, about why we should restore, as well as protect, ecosystems. To put it another way, we can say that restoration of native ecosystems is one of our best treatment modalities for fighting the disease afflicting our planet's biosphere and our grandchildren's future.

Ecosystem restoration often starts and ends with the restoration of the native plant community, and that's especially true of restorations on a smaller scale, which lack the large area required to reintroduce such species as red cockaded woodpeckers, elk, wolves, and bison. Therefore, it's largely a botanical pursuit. But by virtue of the existence of a healthy restored native plant community, there follows an increase in numbers of animal species, such as birds, mammals, reptiles, insects, spiders, and others. Hence the ecosystem with its native biodiversity is, at least in large part, successfully restored.

Restoration ecology follows two important rules of thumb:

1. The larger the area of the ecosystem, the larger the number of species that exist within the ecosystem, and vice versa. This rule follows a mathematical model called insular biogeography equilibrium theory, also known as species–area relationship. For example, if one reduces the area of an ecosystem to one-tenth its original size, that remaining 10 percent of the area will eventually end up with only about 50 percent of the biodiversity of the original ecosystem.[2] Elizabeth Kolbert, in her Pulitzer-winning book *The Sixth Extinction,* gives a highly readable history and explanation of the species–area relationship formula.[3]
2. The larger the number of individuals of a species, the more stable is the population of that species.

These two rules of thumb have particular importance to endemic species (species that exist in a particular area and nowhere else on Earth) and to species in peril. Fragmentation of ecosystems does cause loss of biodiversity, as evidenced by the species–area relationship formula. It should come as no surprise that both of these rules of thumb are important in conservation decision making about, for example, the need to establish corridors to connect a fragmented ecosystem.

The restoration of the shortleaf pine-oak-hickory woodland plant community, as presented in this work, provides a reasonable prototype of an ecological restoration of both a native woodland overstory (the trees) and a native grassland groundcover, which is similar to that of the majority of southern grassland prairies, savannas, and woodlands of the US Midwest and Southeast.

Here I'll begin a discussion of some of the salient features of the shortleaf pine-oak-hickory woodland. This plant community is the foundation of the ecosystem that I am in the process of restoring, a big project in which I've been involved for about a decade and a half.

The shortleaf pine-oak-hickory woodland in historic precolonial times was the dominant plant community of the Upper West Gulf Coastal Plain ecoregion encompassing northwest Louisiana, southwest Arkansas, northeast Texas, and a part of the lands of the Choctaw Nation of southeast Oklahoma.

The map below shows a few of the many ecoregions described in North America. Each is unique, based on a combination of factors such as climate, rainfall, topography, soils, geology, hydrology, flora, fauna, and so forth. The Upper West Gulf Coastal Plain ecoregion comprises gentle rolling hills of mixed pine and hardwoods. Located on the hilltops and upper slopes, it was a fire-sustained woodland instead of a shady forest and was open enough to allow in the sunlight needed to have a grassland groundcover, or what has been described as a "prairie groundcover under trees." Two additional major forest types of this ecoregion (and of Wafer Creek Ranch) are true forests (old-growth, dense, shady, cathedral-like) located downslope along the draws (ravines) and in the bottomlands. My own restoration on Wafer Creek Ranch, where I live, is located in North Louisiana, near Ruston, in Lincoln Parish.

The forest of the draws of the lower slopes of the hills is called the mixed hardwood-loblolly pine forest community, and the forest of the bottomland flood plain is the small-stream forest community. The forest structure of these two communities is quite different from that of the open woodland and its grassland groundcover of the upper slopes and hilltops.

The dominant soil of the uplands of Wafer Creek Ranch can be described as a gravelly fine sandy loam. It is an ultisol, a highly weathered, leached, and acid soil that is very old. It sits upon some of the oldest rock strata in Louisiana, dating back to the Eocene epoch (a division of the Tertiary period, also known as the Paleogene), which extended from about 58 million to 37 million years ago.[4] There are outcrops of Eocene rocks along the slopes of the hills, where I have found a few fascinating plant fossils, making me wonder what that old ecosystem back in those days looked like.

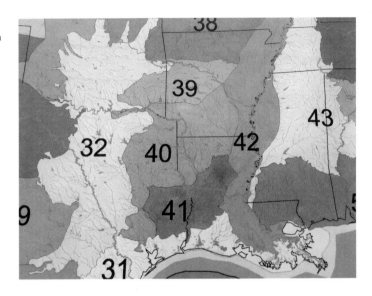

MAP 1. The Upper West Gulf Coastal Plain ecoregion (no. 40) is a region of gentle rolling hills of mixed pine and hardwood. Courtesy The Nature Conservancy, 1999.

One of those Eocene fossils is a large portion of a sizable tree. What species was it? What did it look like? Was it part of a dense forest or a woodland, or did it stand lonely in a savanna? What animals used it for nesting or protection or as a food source? Did it have nest cavities? Did its roots engage in symbiosis with mycorrhizal fungi? If so, did it donate its photosynthetically derived sugar to other members of its species, or to plants of other species? Or both? Did insects visit its flowers, or was it a conifer without true flowers? Did katydids call in its branches in the evening and crickets call for their mates at its base? What was the climate like?

So many questions come to mind, and all seem like the stuff of dreams, yet that tree's environment was a living and breathing ecosystem, a true story lost in the rock strata of the deep past, an ecosystem that thrived in a delicate balance of life and death and of predator and prey once upon a time somewhere between 37 million and 58 million years ago.

THE OVERSTORY OF THE SHORTLEAF PINE-OAK-HICKORY WOODLAND

The overstory consists of relatively fire-resistant trees, as grassland groundcovers are sustained by periodic fires. There are only eight true "card-carrying" members of the shortleaf pine-oak-hickory woodland overstory: the shortleaf pine and seven hardwood species (post oak, white oak, southern red oak, black oak, blackjack oak, mockernut hickory, and black hickory).

Six members of these hardwoods, in addition to the shortleaf pine, can also be found growing downslope along the draws within the mixed hardwood-loblolly pine forest community, which is a shady forest. The one exception is the blackjack oak, which requires abundant sunlight and can thrive only in an open, sunlight-filled woodland or savanna.

The overstory hardwood member trees of this woodland community all have tough bark with deep furrowed ridges, or in the case of the white oak, thick scales or plates. These bark characteristics offer protection from hot fires that rage through the groundcover.

FIG. 2. Post oak, *Quercus stellata.*

FIG. 3. *Above left:* White oak, *Quercus alba.*

FIG. 4. *Above right:* Blackjack oak, *Quercus marilandica.* The lower trunks typically have stiff, down-curved dead limbs, as seen in this photo.

FIG. 5. *Right:* Blackjack oak leaves are club-shaped, kind of like boxing gloves.

Fig. 6. Left: Southern red oak, *Quercus falcata.*

Fig. 7. Below: Black oak, *Quercus velutina.*

FIG. 8. *Right:* Mock-ernut hickory *Carya tomentosa.*

FIG. 9. *Below:* Black hickories, *Carya texana.*

It's easy to see why thin-barked trees such as American beech (*Fagus grandifolia*), American hornbeam (*Carpinus caroliniana*), sweetgum (*Liquidambar styraciflua*), water oak (*Quercus nigra*), red maple (*Acer rubrum*), southern sugar maple (*Acer floridanum*), and winged elm (*Ulmus alata*), which normally grew downslope where fires were cooler burning, could not survive those lightning strike–induced hot fires in the grassland groundcover of the ridges and upper slopes two hundred years ago.

Due to many years of fire suppression, however, the downslope fire-sensitive species have crept uphill, causing the open woodland to become a hybrid shady forest. And that new dark forest effectively shut down the sun-loving woodland grassland that existed in northwest Louisiana so long ago. This is one of the reasons why hot grass fires, not the cooler-burning leaf fires of shady forests, are necessary to sustain a grassy, open woodland.

The aforementioned seven hardwood members are fire-tolerant upland species that can thrive in a hot-fire community of grasses and wildflowers, a grassland-under-the-trees groundcover in open woodland that existed for thousands of years before its demise. Although the overstory species still exist, though in much smaller numbers, the historic woodland plant community (with its grassland groundcover) is now virtually extinct.

It's interesting to realize that most of the landmass of the southeastern United States was actually a grassland before the settlement of people of European descent took its course. But before European settlement, it was for thousands of years home to millions of Native people.

My old friend Latimore Smith is a botanist and restoration scientist recently retired from The Nature Conservancy. Despite his retirement, Latimore continues to be a restoration ecologist extraordinaire, and he's a recipient of the 2018 Environmental Law Institute National Wetlands Award for Conservation and Restoration. I asked Lat how many people he thought even know that the South once was mostly a grassland. He said, "Oh, about fifty-three." Lat was kidding, of course, but the number really is extremely low, even among scientists. Those old grasslands consisted of coastal prairies (2.2 million acres in Louisiana alone!),[5] longleaf pine woodlands and savannas, and upland woodlands such as what dominated the Upper West Gulf Coastal Plain of the Arkansas–Louisiana–Texas region, along with southeastern Oklahoma's Choctaw Nation lands.

The eighth and last member of the shortleaf pine-oak-hickory woodland overstory is the shortleaf pine, *Pinus echinata*. The shortleaf pine is particularly special. It was the grand potentate of the overstory, towering over the fire-resistant oaks and hickories, forming a "supercanopy," as Latimore once described it.

The loblolly pine and the shortleaf pine are the only pine species native to the Upper West Gulf Coastal Plain ecoregion, and both species at adult size are the most fire-resistant tree species—far more fire resistant than the seven hardwood overstory members. So why did the shortleaf survive the periodic hot fires of this woodland grassland but only a paltry few loblolly pines survived? The answer lies at the sapling stage. When fire topkills the saplings, meaning that the saplings are killed by fire from the ground up, the shortleafs will resprout with a healthy, established root system, but the loblollies do not resprout. They've given up the ghost. Fire murders the loblolly babies and spares the shortleaf babies. And this is what gave the shortleaf pine the advantage in a hot-fire plant community.

Shortleaf pines and loblolly pines can be distinguished by their morphology, but sometimes certain trees seem to fall into a gray zone, presenting difficulties even for the experts. A helpful distinguishing feature is the number of needles in a bundle (the small sheath attached to the limb or twig that contains the needles). Usually shortleafs have two-needle bundles (with fewer three-needle bundles) and loblollies have a predominance of three-needle bundles. The bark of old-growth shortleafs have tiny resin pits that extend through the bark plate down to the sapwood. Loblollies have no resin pits. Also, older shortleafs have flat bark plates and loblollies usually have thicker bark plates forming ridges. Shortleafs have shorter needles than those of loblollies, and shortleafs have smaller cones.

Before we move on to the understory groundcover of the woodland, I should mention its midstory, which consisted of shrubs and small trees such as plums (*Prunus spp.*), huckleberry and blueberry (*Vaccinium spp.*), Carolina buckthorn (*Frangula caroliniana*), red buckeye (*Aesculus pavia*), dwarf pawpaw (*Asimina parviflora*), hawthorns (*Crataegus spp.*), and others. But the midstory was a distinctly diminutive level because of the hot fires that rolled through our woodland. Each fire that occurs usually topkills many of the midstory small trees, so they often remain as shrubs.

FIG. 10. *Left:* Resin pits in the flat bark plates of an old-growth short-leaf pine.

FIG. 11. *Below:* Old-growth shortleaf pine, *Pinus echinata.*

THE GROUNDCOVER OF THE
SHORTLEAF PINE-OAK-HICKORY WOODLAND

It was a grassland! I'll get to that. But first a word about some of the North American grasslands of old in the Great Plains.

It's difficult to imagine what it would be like to see and appreciate the vastness of the grassland prairies of the Great Plains, because today they're almost all plowed under and gone. However, there are still a few small remnants, the last holdouts of unplowed prairie—and they are beautiful, historic vistas where the buffalo roamed and Native people followed the herds. Such preserved sites are well worth visiting. The Nature Conservancy protects a 40,000-acre never-plowed tallgrass prairie outside of Pawhuska, Oklahoma; it's open to the public and truly magnificent to see.

In my perhaps oversimplified view, the western third of the Great Plains contained the shortgrass prairie. Moving eastward, that changed over to the mixed tall- and shortgrass prairie, and finally, the eastern third contained the tallgrass prairie.

The tallgrass prairie had multiple species of grasses, but the dominant ones were the "big four": big bluestem, little bluestem, Indiangrass, and switchgrass. It's important to realize that little bluestem was and is a dominant "matrix" species of many tallgrass prairies, savannas, and woodlands west of the Mississippi River, as well as most of the grassland groundcovers on the east side of that great river.

In the centuries before the European invasion, 142 million acres of tallgrass prairie extended from Canada south to the Gulf of Mexico, and at the latitude of northwest Louisiana, it extended eastward to the western edge of East Texas.[6]

But here's the interesting part: the grassland didn't stop there even though the treeless prairie did. Grasslands dominated the landscape of the entire southeastern United States, encompassing coastal prairies, longleaf pine flatwoods and savannas, and upland woodlands.

And something else interesting: the grasslands of the South (along with those of coastal California) are the richest in all of North America, in terms of numbers of species of both plant and certain studied animal groups—much more so than the prairies of the Great Plains. In his book *Hidden Grasslands of the South: Natural History and Conservation* (Island Press, 2013), Reed Noss presents a table comparing five classic prairie plant genera: *Andropogon* (big bluestems), *Sorghastrum* (Indiangrasses), *Schizachyrium* (little bluestems),

Liatris (blazing stars), and *Echinacea* (purple coneflowers). Noss writes, "A simple juxtaposition makes the case: table 1.1 shows species numbers within five classic prairie plant genera of the Prairie region (the Great Plains and Midwest) compared with the South. The South beats the Prairie region hands down." Noss shows the Great Plains/Midwest region as containing two species of the grass genus *Andropogon*.[7] Wafer Creek Ranch has five. The state of Louisiana has eleven. In fact, a significant number of plant species on Wafer Creek Ranch, and shown in this book, are endemic to the South.

So it's true. There really is gold in these old North Louisiana hills. And the farther south we go, the richer in species it gets, until species richness reaches its max along the coast.

I wish I could show you what that shortleaf pine-oak-hickory woodland groundcover looks like, but I can't, because it's virtually extinct.

However, we can come close by checking out the picture of the upland longleaf pine woodland of Kisatchie National Forest in the central part of Louisiana (figure 12). The overstory is different, but the grassland groundcover, dominated by little bluestem, is very similar to what once existed in the historic shortleaf pine-oak-hickory woodland. The grassland groundcover on WCR presently bears little resemblance to this native groundcover in Kisatchie. It will never attain that resemblance until it is dominated by little bluestem, as seen in the photo.

FIG. 12. Kisatchie National Forest longleaf pine woodland dominated by little bluestem. This groundcover is as close as it gets to what the shortleaf pine-oak-hickory woodland groundcover looked like in precolonial times, which is of course the target of the Wafer Creek Ranch restoration. Presently on WCR, little bluestem is far too sparse, making its groundcover appear quite unlike the Kisatchie groundcover in this scene.

Salient Warm Season Grasses of the Woodland Groundcover

FAMILY POACEAE

Members of the grass family likely number around 600 to 700 genera and about 10,000 or more species, making it the fifth-largest flowering plant family. They also are members of the monocot group of plants. Grass stems are hollow except at the nodes and the leaves are alternate, forming a sheath at the leaf's attachment to the stem. The leaf sheath extends below the level of the leaf, wrapping around the stem.

To follow is a list of the salient warm season grasses of the shortleaf pine-oak-hickory woodland. But let us not forget that there are numerous other grass species that are part of the ecosystem, and these few salient grasses shown in this work represent only a few important "poster children" for the system.

I think it's best that we understand that the term "important" might be confusing in this context. What does that mean? For one thing, these grasses are all warm season bunchgrasses that offer the high combustibility needed for those all-important hot fires that are required to sustain the grassland ecosystem. Little bluestem is an exceptionally combustible grass and the dominant grass species in our grassland; therefore, it's the main reason for those hot fires. So, in this case, "important" seems to work.

But the term "important" might be confusing when discussing the concepts of coefficient of conservatism and site floristic quality.

Coefficient of conservatism (C) represents the degree to which a plant species is susceptible to soil disturbance, measured on a scale of zero to 10, with zero being a weedy early successional species and 10 being a species most sensitive to soil disturbance (as exemplified by many late successional and climax species). Plants with a high C-value prefer sites that have had little to no soil disturbance in the recent past. (Nonnative plant species can also be assigned a negative score from –1 to –3 based on their ability to invade and damage a healthy plant community.)

Plants of high C-value, "conservative species," can at times be called "indicator species," because if a site has an abundance of high C-value plants, according to Larry Allain, that site is said to have a high floristic quality. Such a site is considered to be close to what we might have found in grassland groundcovers in precolonial times. On the other hand are the early successional, low C-value species that become weedy in sites of soil disturbance, such as native broomsedge grass, goatweed, false dandelion, and others.

The concepts of coefficient of conservatism and site floristic quality have become important tools in restoration ecology. (Appendix 2 presents a running list of Wafer Creek Ranch grassland species, with C-values for many of the species listed.)

It's probably fair to say that all high C-value plants are "important" in that they represent late successional, if not climax growth in a grassland ecosystem. But is it fair to say that all low C-value plants are not important? Partridge pea, *Chamaecrista fasciculata,* is a fairly low C-value legume, yet it's a nitrogen fixer and a magnificent food source for insects, birds, and mammals, so in this regard it has significant importance as a member of the grassland ecosystem's food web.

When, as guest lecturer, I teach my restoration ecology class to environmental science and entomology students at Louisiana Tech University, I don't use the term "important." I use something that's probably worse: dollar signs. High C-value plants get a $$ label.

Grassland groundcovers of the South, whether in a true prairie or within a savanna or woodland, are living hot spots of biodiversity, containing concentrated numbers of species of plants, reptiles, spiders and scorpions, insects (such as pollinating flies, beetles, bees, and butterflies), birds, mammals, worms, crustaceans, centipedes, mollusks, millipedes, pauropods, springtails, proturans, symphylans, nematodes, tardigrades, fungi, protozoans, and microbes. Unfortunately, little is known about the upland grassland groundcovers of the South because they have been highly degraded or even destroyed in years past, and records with important descriptions are sparse at best.

But a flicker of hope is on the horizon as there are movements to restore these southern biodiverse habitats, and some of them are becoming quite advanced in size and floristic quality. Resurrection of these important long-degraded habitats is labor intensive, time consuming, expensive, and requires expert guidance, but fortunately a small army of dedicated scientists and volunteers (for example, those of the Southeastern Grasslands Initiative and The Nature Conservancy) is on the ground. And that makes me hopeful. Imagine the massive amount of biodiversity recovery for North America that the restoration of the grasslands of the South would accomplish.

Many scientists have traditionally looked to forests as one of the most important natural carbon sinks; thus our reliance on them as a leading force in combating global warming. Yet researchers are showing an increased appreciation for and interest in other sources, such as seagrass meadows, mangrove forests, and salt marshes, as being extremely important players.[1] And we can add to that the role of peatlands of tropical zones as well as those of the Boreal and the Arctic.[2]

Today, grasslands are also coming to light for their importance as carbon sinks, as grasses primarily store their carbon underground in their roots whereas the carbon storage of trees is, for the most part, located in their aboveground structure—the trunks, limbs, leaves, and needles. In this way, grasses don't give up the bulk of their carbon storage when burned, but unfortunately, trees do. With the disastrous wildfires of today, those dry and beetle-damaged forests of the West have become part of a dangerous feedback loop, contributing greenhouse gases to the atmosphere rather than sequestering them.

According to a well-known study by University of California–Davis scientists, in areas that have become extremely fire prone, such as the forests of California and other states in the West, properly managed grasslands are being recognized for the value of their resilience and continued reliability for carbon sequestration in a warming world, so much so that the owners of managed grasslands are being paid through cap-and-trade agreements.[3]

Little bluestem, *Schizachyrium scoparium,* is the dominant "matrix" grass of our shortleaf pine-oak-hickory woodland grassland, just as it is with so many grassland groundcovers, whether in a prairie or a woodland or a savanna of the Midwest and the southeastern states.

Little bluestem is a warm season grass. Grasses are divided into cool season grasses that bloom and go to seed in the spring and warm season grasses that bloom and go to seed in fall, and some grasses (for example, the *Dichantheliums*) are both.

However, it's the warm season grasses that play the dominant role in sustaining the balance of our ecosystem because they form the greatest bulk of combustible biomass needed to sustain the required hot fires. And it is those hot fires that are needed to kill shrub species and other invasive species that might otherwise overtake and smother the grassland. Plus, those hot fires induce bloom and seed production of warm season grasses and wildflowers.[4] Remember: hot fires are what sustain grassland groundcovers.

All the listed salient warm season grasses to follow, including little bluestem, are bunchgrasses. Bunchgrasses grow in a bunch or clump and usually have roots that extend deep into the soil (up to six feet or more), thus providing these grasses with a hardy resistance to drought conditions. They usually are perennials (living more than two years), and they provide excellent habitat and food for insects, mammals, birds, spiders, reptiles, and fungi, such as mycorrhiza that improve soil chemistry and provide nutrients to trees, shrubs, grasses, and wildflowers.

One good example of the advantage of quality habitat pertains to quail. Baby quail cannot walk or run well to escape predators on turf grasses, but they do very well in bunchgrass habitats, where they can quickly scoot on the ground around the clumps of bunchgrass, which provide excellent cover for hiding from predators.

FIG. 13. Notice the dark alley between these bunchgrasses (little bluestem), where quail can run and hide beneath the grass leaves. Hawks are one of nature's biggest threats to quail.

FIG. 14. Little bluestem is the taller, rust-colored bunchgrass in this photo. This grass species needs to dominate the WCR groundcover before our restoration target can be achieved. The scene here also well demonstrates what a typical warm season bunchgrass looks like.

FIG. 15. The inflorescences of little bluestem are the bow-shaped racemes seen here. Each has a row of spikelets that contain the seed. They have a prickly appearance.

Little bluestem, *Schizachyrium scoparium*, is native throughout most of the United States and parts of Mexico and southern Canada and is a fairly high C-value grass. It is a large warm season perennial bunchgrass with a deep fibrous root system and is a dominant grass of the grassland groundcovers of prairies, savannas, and woodlands in most of North America. As a hot-burning bunchgrass, it is the main source of the hot fires of many grassland ecosystems. Little bluestem is host plant to the common wood nymph butterfly and several skipper butterflies: cobweb, Ottoe, Indian, crossline, dusted, and Dixie. Plus, it is a food source for birds and nonlarval insects.[5]

It seems to me the importance of little bluestem's role in the historic woodland grasslands of the Upper West Gulf Coastal Plain cannot be overstated. It was, after all, the dominant grass species and the dominant fire carrier in sustaining those upland grassland ecosystems, and its support for invertebrate and vertebrate species was significant. If little bluestem had, for whatever reason, been removed, would those upland woodland systems have become radically changed or even have survived? I leave that question to the ecologists, but I'm left to wonder whether little bluestem might not have qualified as a keystone species in that shortleaf pine-oak-hickory woodland community of old.

Arrowfeather threeawn, *Aristida purpurascens.* The genus *Aristida* encompasses the threeawn grasses. A grass awn is a little elongate needle or taillike structure attached to the seed head that serves a mechanical function. According to the level of humidity, the awn will coil and uncoil a bit, moving the seed head forward, which increases the chance of bringing it in contact with the ground and thus provides a greater opportunity for germination. As the name threeawn implies, genus *Aristida* has seed spikelets with three awns. Native to the Midwest and eastern North America, arrowfeather threeawn is an example of another, smaller, perennial warm season bunchgrass.[6] Interestingly, the leaves at the plant bases become curly with age, which is said to be a good field mark.[7] The seeds of arrowfeather threeawn are eaten by birds and small rodents.

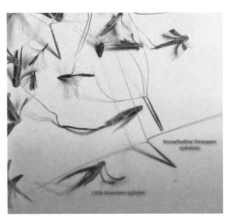

FIG. 17. This photo shows several goldenrod achenes and grass seed spikelets, including little bluestem and Indian grass. But two grass spikelets, one at lower right and one just above it, have three awns—that's arrowfeather threeawn.

FIG. 16. Arrowfeather threeawn, *Aristida purpurascens.* An inflorescence-bearing stem (culm) shows the long needle-like awns of the seed spikelets (each seed spikelet has three). Also notice the curly leaves at the base of this grass—a good field mark.

Splitbeard bluestem, *Andropogon ternarius,* is a large perennial bunchgrass the size of little bluestem. It is one of our most beautiful grasses during the fall, when it has fully developed inflorescences (the bloom and seed heads) that can be seen in figure 18. Splitbeard bluestem has a fibrous root system and grows in the southern Midwest and southeastern portion of North America.[8] The seeds are eaten by small birds and mammals, and the grass is host to wood nymph and skipper butterflies.[9] Bobwhite quail occasionally make their nests in splitbeard bluestem.[10]

FIG. 18. *Above:* Splitbeard bluestem, *Andropogon ternarius.* Notice the fluffy white inflorescences and pink stems (often seen in fall).

FIG. 19. *Right:* Twin racemes of splitbeard bluestem bear fluffy seed spikelets. The racemes separate in two directions, as with an old man's split beard.

Rough dropseed (**hidden dropseed**), *Sporobolus clandestinus,* is a high C-value, occasionally rhizomatous, perennial bunchgrass with a range encompassing the southern Midwest and eastern North America.[11] Sparrows and other small winter birds eat the tiny seeds after they appear in the late fall. In winter the plants are showy and easy to identify as dropseed grass because of the bright, cream-colored leaves and opened sheaths, giving this grass a segmented appearance. It's often called flag grass.

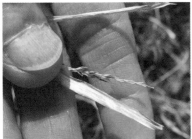

FIG. 20. *Above:* In winter, rough dropseed shows us its bright, open leaves and sheaths. Little bluestem (rust colored, *right*).

FIG. 21. *Left:* Rough dropseed, *Sporobolus clandestinus,* has tiny seed, but birds can find it.

Big bluestem, *Andropogon gerardii,* is a high C-value member of what's called the "big four" grasses, the dominant large perennial bunchgrasses of tallgrass prairie ecosystems. The members of the big four are big bluestem, little bluestem, Indian grass, and switchgrass. Big blue is a large and robust grass of the tallgrass prairie, sometimes reaching up to ten feet or more. Birds and mammals use the grass for cover from predators, and birds make their nests in the plants and eat the seeds. Big blue is a rhizomatous grass and is important in giving the soil a sturdy, erosion-resistant foundation. It's a host plant for several butterfly species.[12] The range of big blue is the Midwest and throughout most of eastern North America.[13]

FIG. 22. *Above:* Big bluestem, *Andropogon gerardii.*

FIG. 23. *Right:* Big bluestem, *Andropogon gerardii.* The raceme inflorescences of big bluestem often come in threes. For this reason, it's sometimes described as resembling a turkey's foot (see the three racemes, *right*).

FIG. 24. Elliott's bluestem, *Andropogon gyrans*. Notice the fanlike spathes containing the fluffy racemes and seed spikelets.

FIG. 25. Slender Indiangrass, *Sorghastrum elliottii*. Notice the droopy seed heads.

Elliott's bluestem, *Andropogon gyrans,* is another high C-value large perennial bunchgrass of our woodland grassland system. It has fibrous roots and its range extends from the southern Midwest and throughout southeastern North America.[14] Its seed is eaten by winter birds during the time when the seed is dispersed, in the late fall and throughout the early winter. These grasses have a distinctive fanlike structure composed of bracts called spathes that open like a fan to expose the inflorescence with its many spikelets that contain the seeds.

Slender Indiangrass, *Sorghastrum elliottii,* is a striking perennial bunchgrass that grows in the southern Midwest and southeastern North America.[15] You will notice in figure 25 that the seed heads appear droopy. That's characteristic of the species and a good field mark. The chestnut brown spikelets and shiny awns are beautiful, making it one of my personal favorites. Slender Indiangrass is a high C-value indicator plant with fibrous roots. Its cousin, yellow Indiangrass (*Sorghastrum nutans*), is a member of the big four grasses of tallgrass prairies.

FIG. 26. Purple lovegrass, *Eragrostis spectabilis*.

Purple lovegrass, *Eragrostis spectabilis,* is another warm season rhizomatous perennial bunchgrass with a delicate, cloud-like display of purple panicle inflorescences (the floral and seed heads).[16] The inflorescences become detached later in the year and tumble along on the ground in the wind, reminiscent of tumbleweeds.[17] The range of purple lovegrass extends from northern Mexico into the Midwest and eastern North America.[18] It is a food source for birds and insects and a host plant for the Zabulon skipper butterfly.[19] As the restoration matures over time and the large bunchgrasses such as little bluestem take their dominant role, purple lovegrass may become relegated to having a fairly minor role in the system. Another, larger lovegrass on WCR is lacegrass, *Eragrostis capillaris.* It is an annual with exaggerated panicles that also roll like tumbleweeds in the winter wind when detached from the plant.

Bentawn plumegrass, *Saccharum brevibarbe var. contortum,* or *Erianthus contortus* (Elliott). A specimen from WCR has been identified by Chris Doffitt, a botanist with the Louisiana Department of Wildlife and Fisheries (LDWF). Chris used two keys—*Flora of North America,* for the first name, and Allen Weakley's *Flora of the Southeastern United States: Louisiana* (2022), for the second.[20] Weakley's key came up *Erianthus contortus* (Elliott). Taxonomically, the two scientific names are synonymous: bentawn plumegrass. (This is an example of just how messy taxonomy can get, and not only for plants.) It's interesting that the very similar **silver plumegrass**, *S. alopecuroides,* has also been identified in the North Louisiana hill country. These wild plumegrasses are cousins of the commercially grown sugarcane that falls under the same genus, *Saccharum.* Our native plumegrasses have large, fluffy, brownish to cream-colored to silvery plumes and grow up to thirteen feet tall or more. They are perennial bunchgrasses that have fibrous roots and grow well in sunny, dry uplands. Bentawn plumegrass is a Deep South species that ranges from Texas eastward to the Atlantic.[21] Plumegrasses provide good cover for birds and mammals, and they often are host plants to the common wood nymph and clouded skipper butterflies.[22]

FIG. 27. *Left:* Bentawn plumegrass, *Saccharum brevibarbe var. contortum.*

Narrow plumegrass, *Saccharum strictus,* also growing on Wafer Creek Ranch, shares many of the features of bentawn plumegrass except that the plumes are more restricted and without bentawn's fluffiness. Additionally, the plumes of narrow plumegrass are somewhat browner, having a drab appearance.[23]

FIG. 28. *Above:* Narrow plumegrass, *Saccharum strictus.* Notice the inflorescence of this species is more restricted and brownish, lacking the bright, creamy fluffiness seen with the plumes of bentawn plumegrass.

FIG. 29. Gulf Coast (pink) muhlygrass, *Muhlenbergia capillaris.* Photo credit: Larry Allain, US Geological Survey.

Gulf Coast (pink) muhlygrass, *Muhlenbergia capillaris,* is a warm season non-rhizomatous perennial bunchgrass with a native range encompassing parts of Mexico and Central America and the southern Midwest and eastern United States.[24] In the fall the seed spikelets turn purple, giving the inflorescence a pink-lavender hue. It is known as an indicator of calcareous soil but it also seems to do well in Wafer Creek Ranch's acid, dry-mesic soil. However, it is uncommon on WCR. Muhly provides cover for small birds, and mammals eat the seeds.[25]

A FEW OTHER WARM SEASON GRASSES ON WAFER CREEK RANCH

The following are a few more representative grass species that populate sites of soil disturbance. Nevertheless, we must remember that all the natives have value in the ecosystem, and they are good fire carriers.

Bird-beaked panicum, *Panicum anceps,* is a common, low C-value perennial bunchgrass and a good carrier of fire, thus making it a species of value for the restoration and maintenance of the grassland ecosystem. The seeds are curved, reminiscent of a bird's beak. The plant's rhizomes have sites of active cell growth, called meristems, that form beak-like structures that often will become a new plant. Botanists sometimes refer to them as cock's spurs. Being that the plant is rhizomatous, it often occurs in clusters and it tends to prefer zones of dampness. It is browsed by deer, and birds eat the seeds in late fall and winter. Its range extends from the Midwest throughout the southeastern United States.[26]

FIG. 30. Bird-beaked panicum, *Panicum anceps.*

FIG. 31. Purpletop grass, *Tridens flavus.*
Photo credit: Jeff McMillian, Almost Eden.

Purpletop grass, *Tridens flavus,* is a warm season perennial bunchgrass of low C-value. It has purple seeds that have a greasy texture, giving the species the additional common name of greasegrass. Purpletop is host plant for the common wood nymph and several skipper butterflies.[27] Purpletop's range is throughout the Midwest and eastern United States.[28]

FIG. 32. Prairie threeawn grass, *Aristida oligantha.*

Prairie threeawn grass, *Aristida oligantha,* is a warm season annual grass of low C-value; therefore, it can become weedy in sites of soil disturbance. Its range extends throughout most of the United States. Small mammals use the grass as nesting sites and sometimes move the grass to line their nests. Birds eat the seeds.[29] The awns of this grass are sometimes quite long, about 2.5 inches.[30]

FIG. 33. Broomsedge grass, *Andropogon virginicus.*

Broomsedge grass, *Andropogon virginicus,* is a perennial clump-forming bunchgrass. Its seeds are easily carried by wind and are spread over large areas. Additionally, the seeds have a high germination rate. Broomsedge can thrive in disturbed soils, as expected for a weedy species. Characteristic of the large bunchgrasses, broomsedge is a good fire carrier, and the grass is a food source for deer, and particularly for birds in winter. I have personally watched small flocks of chipping sparrows seemingly enjoying themselves while riding down the stems (culms) to get to the seeds. The range of broomsedge is the Midwest, eastern United States, and into Canada.[31]

FIG. 34. Bushy broomsedge, *Andropogon glomeratus.*

FIG. 35. Longleaf woodoats, *Chasmanthium sessiliflorum* or slender woodoats, *Chasmanthium laxum.*

Bushy bluestem (or **bushy broomsedge**), *Andropogon glomeratus,* is an impressive large perennial bunchgrass preferring moist soils. Its tufted inflorescences stand out, making this species easy to identify, but in certain sites, bushy bluestem can become weedy. It has value in the ecosystem as a good fire carrier and provider of nesting material for birds and cover for both birds and mammals. The seeds provide food for winter bird species such as sparrows and juncos, and it is occasionally browsed by larger mammals. Bushy bluestem is host plant for common wood nymph, skipper, and satyr butterflies.[32] The plant's native range encompasses Central America, Mexico, and most of the southern half of the United States.[33]

Longleaf woodoats and slender woodoats, *Chasmanthium sessiliflorum* and *Chasmanthium laxum,* are similar-appearing dwarf shade-tolerant grasses that grow well in partially shaded upland woodland settings as well as in full sun. These warm season grasses, both of which thrive on Wafer Creek Ranch, are drought-tolerant perennials with a range extending across the southern Midwest and eastern United States, primarily along the Gulf and Atlantic coastal plain.[34] Deer browse the leaves and stems and birds eat the seeds.[35]

Velvet panicgrass, *Dichanthelium scoparium,* is a perennial rhizomatous grass that, like so many other *Dichanthelium* species, produces a basal rosette of green leaves that lasts over winter. In spring and summer, the grass stems

FIG. 36. Velvet panic-grass, *Dichanthelium scoparium*. The plant here is in the profusely branching, late summer (autumnal) growth stage.

grow, profusely branch, and produce their longer leaves and their inflorescences. The *Dichantheliums* have two bloom phases over the year. Velvet panicgrass is the largest *Dichanthelium* species on Wafer Creek Ranch. Its leaves and stems are soft and velvety, hence the common name. The species seems to thrive best in full sun. Velvet panicgrass has a native range encompassing part of Mexico, the southern Midwest, and the southeastern United States. The species is an important seed source for birds and small mammals, and deer and turkey browse the leafy rosettes in winter.[36]

Forbs and Other Nongrass Species of the Shortleaf Pine-Oak-Hickory Woodland Groundcover

Forbs are nongrass, nonwoody plants, which means that they are not trees, shrubs, woody vines, or graminoids (grasses, sedges, and rushes). On the other hand, herbaceous plants include both the forbs and the graminoids.

Wildflowers of the grassland ecosystem are mainly forbs. As members of the food web, wildflowers are foundational in that they are strongly supportive of animals, especially insects, by providing them with nectar and pollen. As well, many forbs serve as host plants for insect larvae and many nonlarval insects feed on the leaves, stems, and roots of forbs. We should remember that insects are a necessary (if not the only) food source for a great many species, including numerous birds, small mammals, freshwater fish, reptiles, amphibians, predatory insects, spiders, and others.

So this begins to give us a glimpse of just how important wildflowers are to the food web within the ecosystem, and just how interdependent all species are. Ecosystems are layered, looped, and richly interconnected in profound and mostly undiscovered ways.

There are a few other wildflower species in the following descriptions that are not herbaceous wildflowers. For example, coral bean is technically a shrub. Also, because of its fascinating biology as a symbiont with mycorrhiza, I was unable to resist the temptation to include Indian pipe, which doesn't qualify as a grassland species because it requires essentially no sunlight.

FAMILY AGAVACEAE: AGAVES AND YUCCAS

In the group of monocots, this family contains some of the well-known succulent plants of dry zones, such as the agaves and yuccas. There are about twenty-three genera and around 640 species located in subtropical and warm temperate areas worldwide. They often occur as succulents, meaning the plant parts are thick and fleshy from water retention. Cacti, which are dicots, are also good examples of succulent plants. Typical of most monocots, the leaf veins are parallel. Some botanists refer to the "true" agaves as those plants that die when they bloom, such as for example, the century plant. The agaves on Wafer Creek Ranch, eastern agave and yucca, are annually blooming perennials.

Eastern agave, *Manfreda virginica,* is a rhizomatous perennial forb member of the monocot group.[1] Its range is the southern Midwest and eastern United States.[2] These high C-value plants have long, lance-like leaves that form a rosette. From the leafy rosette a flower stalk can grow to eight feet tall. The highly fragrant tubular flowers eventually form green, globe-shaped seed capsules. Flower pollination is mostly nocturnal, by sphinx moths, and to a lesser degree by bees during the daytime.[3] On Wafer Creek Ranch the plants seem to favor well-drained upland woodland habitats with partial shade.

FIG. 37. Eastern agave, *Manfreda virginica.*
Notice the leafy rosette.

FIG. 38. *Top right:* The fragrant tubular flowers of eastern agave.

FIG. 39. *Bottom right:* Eastern agave, *Manfreda virginica.* The top of the stalk demonstrates one to several three-celled seed capsules, as shown here.

FIG. 40. Yucca in bloom on Wafer Creek Ranch.

Beargrass yucca, *Yucca louisianensis* or *Yucca filimentosa*. Both species can occur in Lincoln Parish, but *louisianensis* is most likely the species on Wafer Creek Ranch.[4] They are perennial, rhizomatous plants (often considered shrubs) and members of the monocots. *Yucca louisianensis* has a North American range restricted in the United States to Louisiana, Texas, Arkansas, and four counties of the southeastern portion of the Choctaw Nation of Oklahoma, whereas *Yucca filimentosa*'s range encompasses the Midwest and much of the eastern United States.[5] The plants grow tall, up to eight feet (the flower clusters alone may reach a length of up to three feet). In some regions, moths, such as the yucca moth, are yucca pollinators and use yucca flowers (other than those pollinated) for their host by depositing eggs on the flower. Here, the moth caterpillars can eventually eat the seed, their food source. Hummingbirds also gather nectar from the flowers, and the plant is host to skipper butterflies.[6] The plants prefer dry sites and full sun but are partially shade tolerant.

FAMILY COMMELINACEAE: DAYFLOWERS

The dayflower family, a member of the monocot group, is large, having more than 700 known species and about forty genera. The family is most diverse in both Old World and New World tropics.

Virginia spiderwort, *Tradescantia virginiana,* is a perennial forb that is quite shade tolerant, but it can tolerate more lengthy periods of sunlight if the ground is moist. Individual flowers on a plant last for only one day, but blooming is staggered during the day so that the plant still has blooms as its flowers die. The flowers attract bees (the plant's principal pollinators), butterflies, and other insects seeking pollen.[7] Deer and rabbits browse the leaves.[8] Virginia spiderwort's range in North America is the southern Midwest and eastern United States.[9]

FIG. 41. Virginia spiderwort, *Tradescantia virginiana.*

FAMILY LAMIACEAE: MINTS

Lamiaceae, the family of mints, has a cosmopolitan distribution with more than 200 genera and nearly 7,000 species and includes such culinary plants as rosemary, sage, basil, spearmint, oregano, hyssop, thyme, perilla, and lavender. Mints may exist as herbaceous plants, shrubs, or trees (such as teak). The largest genus in the family is *Salvia*.

Mints have square stems and are often aromatic. They frequently have beautiful blooms, making them important for animals attracted to nectar and pollen. Fortunately, they are quite common in our woodland grassland system on Wafer Creek Ranch.

Wild bergamot, *Monarda fistulosa,* is a striking high C-value perennial forb with a large distribution throughout North America. Known as one of the beebalms, it is a late spring– to early summer–blooming mint in Louisiana. Wild bergamot blooms are spectacular and excellent attractants for many insects, including such pollinators as bees, butterflies, wasps, flies, and even hummingbirds.[10] It's also host plant to several moth species. Wild bergamot is a rhizomatous forb often occurring in clumps of multiple plants.[11]

FIG. 42. Pipevine swallowtail butterfly on wild bergamot, *Monarda fistulosa,* a mecca for pollinators.

FIG. 43. Spotted beebalm, *Monarda punctata*. Because this photo was taken in November, it's likely the monarch here is a fourth-generation specimen on its way to the highlands of central Mexico. It will spend the winter there, and in the following spring it will travel north, breed and (if it's a female) lay its eggs on milkweed, thus giving birth to the new season's first generation.

Spotted beebalm, *Monarda punctata,* is another native perennial mint and pollen and nectar provider. The words "spotted" and "punctate" refer to the spots on the yellow tubular flowers that are being visited by the monarch in figure 43. It was passing through in November, presumably on its way to the oyamel fir forests located in the highlands of central Mexico and making this pit stop in an effort to build up its energy resources. Spotted beebalm is common in central and eastern North America.[12] The plant can spread by stolon-like runners forming plant colonies.

Azure blue sage, *Salvia azurea,* is an impressive, erect (up to six feet tall) perennial mint of our woodland. It has a high C-value with a range centered in the Midwest, but from there the range extends rather far eastward and westward.[13] The leaves are elongate and usually slightly serrated, and the stems are long, uniform, and squared (though occasionally only minimally). Many of the plants are also somewhat minimally aromatic for a mint. The flowers are important nectar and pollen sources for insects and hummingbirds, and azure blue sage serves as host to the hermit sphinx moth.[14]

FIG. 44. Azure blue sage, *Salvia azurea.*

Whiteleaf mountain mint, *Pycnanthemum albescens,* is a striking perennial forb mint with fibrous roots. Its crushed leaves produce a unique, sweet minty aroma and it has been used as a spice in cooking. Because of its fragrance and the distinguished frost-colored leaves and bracts supporting its interesting blossoms, whiteleaf mountain mint is one of my favorite wildflowers. It must be so for insects, too, as the blossoms are often busy with buzzing insects and other pollinators. The range of whiteleaf mountain mint is the southern Midwestern and Eastern coastal states of North America.[15]

FIG. 45. Whiteleaf mountain mint, *Pycnanthemum albescens.* Notice the frost-colored leaves and bracts supporting the flowers.

FIG. 46. Narrowleaf mountain mint, *Pycnanthemum tenuifolium,* shown with a pearl crescent butterfly gathering nectar. Upper wing surface in view. Butterfly identification thanks to Chris Carlton, entomologist Louisiana State University, Baton Rouge.

Narrowleaf mountain mint, *Pycnanthemum tenuifolium,* is a rhizomatous perennial forb of the mint family. It grows to about three feet in height and thrives in full sun or partial shade within well-drained soil. The plants provide pollen and nectar to hummingbirds, bees, butterflies, wasps and other insects, and deer graze the leaves. The seeds are eaten by small mammals and birds.[16] The plant's range is the Midwest and eastern United States.[17]

FIG. 47. Bluecurls, *Trichostema dichotomum.*

Bluecurls, *Trichostema dichotomum,* an annual forb, is a striking plant due to its flowers having long stamens (male reproductive organs consisting of anthers and filaments) that curl over the female parts of the flower. Its range extends from the southern Midwest and throughout the eastern United States.[18] It prefers partial shade in dry woodland settings. The flowers provide pollen and nectar for bees and other insects.[19]

FAMILY APIACEAE: PARSLEY

This family contains about 3,700 species and about 434 genera. It includes such well-known plants as parsley, carrot, fennel, anise, celery, cumin, dill, parsnip, and coriander. Some of these plants have blossoms resembling umbrellas, such as wild carrot of the *Daucus* genus. The inflorescences are composed of many similar small flowers with stems emanating from the same point—somewhat like the ribs of an umbrella. Often these arrangements are flat-topped.

Rattlesnake master, *Eryngium yuccifolium,* is a high C-value distinctive perennial species of tallgrass prairies and other grasslands of the Midwest and the eastern United States.[20] It grows up to five feet tall and is one of the few dicots that has parallel veins in its leaves. Rattlesnake master attracts many insect pollinators, such as bees, butterflies, beetles, flies, and especially wasps. It is host plant for the rattlesnake master stem borer moth and the seed-eating moth, and it's an occasional host for the black swallowtail butterfly. Rattlesnake master was used by Native peoples for weaving. However, there is a religious sect of "snake handlers" who engage in the dangerous practice of rattlesnake ceremony. The snake handlers believe that parts of the plant are protective in their interaction with the snakes. I don't buy it, myself. But regardless of its curious origin, I think "rattlesnake master" is a cool name for this plant.[21]

FIG. 48. Rattlesnake master, *Eryngium yuccifolium.*

FAMILY FABACEAE: LEGUMES

The legumes represent an exceptionally important family of plants for the woodland grassland, as they are beneficial for both animals and plants alike. In this regard, they produce nectar and pollen from the flowers for insects, and protein from the peas and beans for other animals such as mammals and birds. The foliage is also browsed by mammals and birds, such as wild turkeys. Legume seeds tend to hold their protein content longer than the seeds of grasses and other forbs in late winter, which is beneficial to animals in that season.

Legumes also benefit plants, enriching the soil by their symbiotic relationship with nitrogen-fixing bacteria (rhizobia and other bacteria) within the legumes' root nodules. The bacteria take nitrogen from the air and convert it to ammonium and other nitrogenous compounds usable by plants, including by the host legume itself.

Legumes represent the third-largest terrestrial plant family on Earth, following the orchid and sunflower families.

Coral bean, *Erythrina herbacea,* is one of the showiest bloomers on Wafer Creek Ranch. Known as Mamou in south Louisiana, other common names include coral bean and Cherokee bean. Its range extends from eastern Mexico, coastal Texas, and Louisiana to South Carolina and Florida, for the most part hugging the coastal states. Coral bean blossoms are a source of pollen and nectar for hummingbirds and long-tongued insects, and small mammals use the plants as cover.[22] The shiny bright-red beans are highly toxic to humans. In North Louisiana, coral bean grows like a perennial forb from tuberous roots in the spring, but it's actually a shrub that dies back due to its sensitivity to freezing in winter. Farther south it will live through the winter as a shrub or small tree.

FIG. 49. Coral bean,
Erythrina herbacea.

FIG. 50. 2.53.
Desmodium species.

Desmodium is the genus for a number of species which, unfortunately, I cannot sort out. But many botanists also have difficulty sorting out all the species in this complicated genus. There are close to 700 species of *Desmodium* worldwide, and around seventy or more species are native to the United States. The multiple species on Wafer Creek Ranch are robust nitrogen-fixing plants with flowers that provide nectar and pollen for insects, and their segmented bean pods (loments) are an important food source for birds and mammals. Also, *Desmodium* is a host plant for certain butterfly species.

FIG. 51. *Desmodium* bean pods (loments) on a very large *Desmodium* leaflet.

I think we are all familiar with some *Desmodium* members, if only because they are the source of the beggar's lice (sticktights) on our clothes after we've entered a weedy area in fall. Perhaps we shouldn't be surprised as the plants of this genus have little pink flowers that stick their tongues out at us.

Dollarleaf, *Desmodium rotundifolium,* is also called prostrate (or trailing) ticktrefoil. It is a native legume and perennial vine-like forb with trailing stems three to six feet long. It has pink flowers and prefers dry sites in partial

FIG. 52. Dollarleaf,
Desmodium rotundifolium.

to almost full shade. Dollarleaf's range is the southern Midwest, eastern United States, and Ontario.[23] It is imperiled in Ontario and Kansas. Deer and birds (including turkey, bobwhite quail, and ruffed grouse) and small mammals eat the loments of dollarleaf.[24] Insects gather the flower nectar and pollen.

Bush (hairy) lespedeza, *Lespedeza hirta,* is a large (up to five feet tall) and showy perennial forb. The lespedezas are often upright, largely unbranching, vertical growing legumes, giving the plants a sometimes narrow conformation. But bush lespedeza does demonstrate branching, which gives the plant a bushy appearance. It has inconspicuous white flowers.[25] As with many but not all legumes, their leaflets grow in threes (trifoliate). Bush lespedeza has a large range extending from Canada south through the southeastern United States and the Midwest.[26] The plant is special in that it serves as larval host plant to several moth and butterfly species, including the cloudless sulphur and gray hairstreak. Plus, it's a good pollen and nectar provider for insects and its seeds and foliage are important to birds and mammals.[27]

FIG. 53. Bush
lespedeza,
Lespedeza hirta.

FIG. 54. Slender lespedeza, *Lespedeza virginica.*

Slender lespedeza, *Lespedeza virginica,* is a native perennial forb that can stand three to six feet tall. It has pink to lavender flowers and the leaflets are narrow and elongate. The stems are long and largely unbranching, and the plant has a deep taproot, giving slender lespedeza drought resistance. It prefers dry, well-drained soils in full sun or the partial shade of woodlands. The flowers provide nectar and pollen to insects, such as bees, flies, wasps, and butterflies. Slender lespedeza is host plant to skipper butterflies, including northern and southern cloudywing and hoary edge skipper. Several bird species eat the seed, and mammals such as deer and rabbits browse the plants.[28] The range of slender lespedeza is the southern Midwest, eastern United States, and Ontario.[29]

Pink fuzzybean, *Strophostyles umbellata.* A presentation of the grassland plant community could hardly exclude the little pink fuzzybean. The plant's bright pink flower is distinctive, having a somewhat umbrella shape and a twisted, hook-like keel. Common in the southeast and southern Midwest, the flowers of pink fuzzybean are pollen and nectar sources for insects and the beans are food for bobwhite quail.[30] Pink fuzzybean is a good example of a perennial legume forb that grows as a vine.

FIG. 55. Pink fuzzybean, *Strophostyles umbellata.*

FIG. 56. *Above:*
Partridge pea, *Chamae-
crista fasciculata,*
responds well to the
periodic fires of the
woodland.

FIG. 57. *Right:* Partridge
pea with its numerous
pea pods.

Partridge pea, *Chamaecrista fasciculata,* is a common native annual legume throughout most of the Midwest and eastern North America.[31] The flower is pollinated only by long-tongued bees such as bumblebees and honeybees. Though the flowers produce pollen only, the leaf stems serve as extrafloral nectaries where a different set of insects, including ants, halictid bees, flies, and wasps, can gather the nectar.[32] Though partridge pea is a low C-value forb, it is very important in the ecosystem as it produces nectar and pollen for insects and the pea pods are an excellent winter food source for birds and mammals. Partridge pea stands two to three feet tall and each plant produces many pea pods. The plant is host for several species of butterfly, including two species of sulphur.

Climbing (or spurred) butterfly pea, *Centrosema virginianum,* is a common native perennial forb and nitrogen fixer. It thrives in open, sunny areas and its native range includes the central and southern United States west to Texas, and south to Mexico, Central America, South America, and the West Indies.[33] It's a vine legume and is an excellent food source for wildlife because of its nectar and pollen, which are consumed by bees and other insects, and its elongate seedpods provide seed, which are eaten by birds and mammals.

FIG. 58. *Left:* Climbing butterfly pea, *Centrosema virginianum.* The floral banner of the flower is the deflated football–like appendage curling toward the flower's center. Bumblebees go under it to get nectar and pollen, and I often can see only their butts (abdomens) sticking out before they decide to back out and buzz off to another flower.

FIG. 59. Sensitive briar, *Mimosa nuttallii,* with its pink pompom flowers.

FIG. 60. Sensitive briar showing its starfish seedpods.

Sensitive briar (catclaw briar), *Mimosa nuttallii,* is a creeping, prickly vine legume of the Midwestern states.[34] It's a nitrogen-fixing perennial important as a source of nectar and pollen for insects, and the leaves and seeds are a protein source for birds such as bobwhite quail. The plants exhibit seismonasty, meaning the leaves are sensitive to touch, wind, and darkness, which trigger the leaflets to fold.[35] The flowers are interesting pink pompoms and the seedpods are unique, forming prickly starfish arrangements.

Goat's rue, *Tephrosia virginiana,* is a high C-value perennial legume forb of the Midwest and eastern North America.[36] The beans provide a food source for birds and mammals. Insects gather the pollen and nectar, and several species of insect use it as a larval host plant. However, the plant is toxic to some insects, livestock, and fish as it contains rotenone.[37] Goat's rue is a deep-taprooted species. Unfortunately, examples of this plant are quite rare on Wafer Creek Ranch today, but it would have existed in larger numbers in the grassland during historic times.

FIG. 61. *Right:* Goat's rue, *Tephrosia virginiana.* My copilot, Opal, in the background.

FIG. 62. *Below:* Twining snoutbean, *Rhynchosia tomentosa,* with its beans.

Twining snoutbean, *Rhynchosia tomentosa,* is a nitrogen fixer and an upright-climbing high C-value perennial forb. It has yellow flowers that produce beans in the fall, which should serve as a good food source for wildlife. On Wafer Creek Ranch, twining snoutbean seems to prefer upland sites. The plant's range is the southern Midwest and the southeastern United States.[38]

FIG. 63. Prairie snoutbean, *Rhynchosia latifolia,* with its beans.

Prairie snoutbean, *Rhynchosia latifolia,* is another high C-value twining vine with broader leaves than *R. tomentosa.* It also prefers upland sites on Wafer Creek Ranch. Like *tomentosa,* it has yellow flowers and beans that should provide an important food source for insects, birds, and mammals. It is a nitrogen-fixing perennial forb native to the southern Midwest and south-central states.[39]

FIG. 64. Pencil flower, *Stylosanthes biflora.*

Sidebeak pencil flower, *Stylosanthes biflora,* is a small erect perennial legume forb whose yellow flowers provide pollen and nectar for insects, and its leaves and seeds are eaten by birds, deer, and small mammals.[40] Pencil flower is host plant to a leaf beetle, *Sumitrosis ancoroides.*[41] The range of the plant is the southern Midwest and the eastern United States.[42]

Downey milkpea, *Galactia volubilis,* is a long, twining perennial forb and native legume vine. Common in the southern Midwest and eastern United States, it serves as browse for both large and small mammals and the seeds are eaten by birds and small rodents.[43] Downey milkpea has three leaflets and small pink flowers and can form dense tangles by twining around other plants.

FIG. 65. Downey milkpea, *Galactia volubilis.*

FAMILY APOCYNACEAE, SUBFAMILY ASCLEPIADOIDEAE: MILKWEED

The milkweed subfamily contains more than 400 genera distributed almost worldwide. Our milkweeds of genus *Asclepias,* which exist in the North American temperate zones, are forbs with toxic sap in the stems and leaves. The sap contains cardenolide, which is poisonous to most animals other than milkweed insects. Although the milkweed toxin consumed by the larval monarch butterfly is largely protective against predators for both larvae and adults, exceptions include the blackheaded grossbeak and the Mexican endemic blackheaded oriole, which have adapted to eating monarch butterflies. However, neither of these bird species occur in the Upper West Gulf Coastal Plain. Milkweeds serve as the larval hosts for a variety of milkweed bugs (such as the large milkweed bug) and milkweed beetles (such as the red milkweed beetle), the imperiled monarch butterfly, the queen butterfly, and the tussock moth.[44]

So far, three milkweed species of genus *Asclepias* have been identified on Wafer Creek Ranch: **white-flowered milkweed**, *Asclepias variegata;* **blunt-leaf milkweed**, *A. amplexicaulis;* and **butterfly milkweed**, *A. tuberosa.* Of the three species, the shade-tolerant white-flowered milkweed is the most common and is increasing its numbers in the restoration, thus raising more and more monarch butterflies—a good example of restoration effecting the rescue of our vanishing biodiversity, and in this case, an imperiled species.

FIG. 66. White-flowered milkweed, *Asclepias variegata,* the most common milkweed on Wafer Creek Ranch.

The range of these three milkweed species includes the Midwest and eastern North America.[45] The extravagant blossoms are fair game for many animals other than milkweed insects and are important pollen and nectar sources for flies, wasps, beetles, bees, butterflies, and hummingbirds.

FIG. 67. *Left:* Monarch caterpillar on white-flowered milkweed.

FIG. 68. *Below:* Seed pod of white-flowered milkweed releasing its seeds to the wind.

FIG. 69. *Above:* Butterfly milkweed, *Asclepias tuberosa,* has tuberous roots.

FIG. 70. *Right:* Blunt-leaf milkweed, *Asclepias amplexicaulis.*

FIG. 71. Anglepod, *Matelea gonocarpos.* The smooth surface of the pod in this photo is a diagnostic field mark.

Anglepod (old field milkvine), *Matelea gonocarpos,* is a woodland vine of the milkweed subfamily that grows in both sunny and partially shady sites. It has milky sap and its seeds strongly resemble those of white-flowered milkweed, *Asclepias variegata.* The smooth surface of the fruit (seedpod) is a diagnostic field mark of this species as the other members of genus *Matelea* have pods with spiny surface projections.[46] The flowers of anglepod are usually small, greenish-yellow, and star-shaped. The range of anglepod extends from the southern Midwest throughout the southeastern United States. Interestingly, within the United States, the densest population appears to be in Louisiana, as it is present in the vast majority of parishes but identified only within scattered counties of other states.[47] Anglepod is host to monarch butterflies, milkweed bugs, and tussock moth.[48] Butterflies, bees, and other insects gather nectar and pollen from its flowers.

FIG. 72. Climbing milkvine, *Matelea decipiens.*

Climbing milkvine, *Matelea decipiens,* is often called old field milkvine, which is confusing as we often give anglepod the same name. Its range is the southern Midwest and eastern states. It is presently listed as critically imperiled in Kansas, Illinois, and Virginia. In Louisiana and several other states, its conservation status is unranked.[49] The purple flowers of the plant in figure 72 were diagnostic for speciation by Louisiana Department of Wildlife and Fisheries botanist Chris Doffitt. The seedpods of climbing milkvine have spiny surfaces.

FAMILY EUPHORBIACEAE: SPURGES

The spurge family is large, comprising more than 200 genera and more than 6,000 species. The fruit of many of our species are capsules (schizocarps) that split open, scattering the seeds. In North America, the family members primarily exist as forbs, but the spurges have a worldwide distribution, with most in the tropical zones, where they exist as forbs, shrubs, or trees. Due to the fascinating phenomenon of convergent evolution, some species strongly resemble cacti, but they are far removed from the cactus family. Convergent evolution is the evolutionary process by which species may show a strong anatomical resemblance and occupy similar ecological niches, behaviors, and roles though they are not related and have widely separate ancestral backgrounds. The classic example is the Tasmanian wolf and the gray wolf, which bear a strong resemblance to each other both ecologically and morphologically. However, the Tasmanian wolf is a marsupial mammal and the gray wolf is a placental mammal. They have no kinship except very far back in early mammalian evolution.

Flowering spurge, *Euphorbia corollata*, is a high C-value species that exists as a small plant on Wafer Creek Ranch. It's a somewhat shade-tolerant perennial forb that has toxic sap. On Wafer Creek Ranch, flowering spurge seems to prefer well-drained upland woodland settings. It has a deep taproot, giving the plants drought tolerance. Its range is the Midwest and throughout the eastern United States to southern Ontario. The flowers attract pollinating insects such as bees, wasps, flies, and butterflies, and birds eat the seeds.[50] The plant's bloom period is late spring, summer, and fall.

FIG. 73. Flowering spurge, *Euphorbia corollata,* with its white flowers.

FIG. 74. Nettleleaf noseburn, *Tragia urticifolia.*
Notice the seed capsules near the top of the plant.

FIG. 75. Texas bullnettle, *Cnidoscolus texanus.*

Nettleleaf noseburn, *Tragia urticifolia,* is a perennial forb that has a range almost completely restricted to the Southern Gulf Coast states from Texas eastward.[51] On Wafer Creek Ranch it seems almost always restricted to dry upland woodland sites, where it occurs as a small plant. Noseburn causes itching when it comes in contact with the skin; hence its name.

Texas bullnettle, *Cnidoscolus texanus,* is a high C-value[52] perennial forb with stinging hairs; therefore, touching it is not a great idea. Its range is restricted to the state of Tamaulipas, Mexico, and the states of Texas, Louisiana, Arkansas, Oklahoma, and Kansas. Insects such as bees and butterflies feed on the nectar and pollen of the showy white flowers, and birds eat the seeds. The seeds are also edible for humans and were a part of the diet of Native peoples.[53] Texas bullnettle has a deep taproot and is quite drought resistant. It is an indicator of sandy soil.

Goatweed (**woolly croton, hogwort**), *Croton capitatus,* is a highly weedy invader of disturbed sites. It is an annual plant with velvety-textured leaves and stems due to the plant's hairs (trichomes). The seeds are eaten by birds and the plant is host to the gray hairstreak and goatweed leafwing butterflies, *Anaea andria.*[54] The goatweed leafwing is a large, beautiful butterfly fairly common in the warm months on Wafer Creek Ranch, causing me to realize that the weedy goatweed, after all, has significant worth in the ecosystem. The range of goatweed is centered in the southern Midwestern states. Farther east it becomes scattered and local.[55]

FIG. 76. *Left:* Goatweed, *Croton capitatus.* Notice the seed capsules typical of many members of Euphorbiaceae.

FIG. 77. *Below:* Vente conmigo, *Croton glandulosus.*

Vente conmigo, *Croton glandulosus,* is an annual forb preferring sunny locations, but it tolerates partial shade. *Vente conmigo* is Spanish for "come with me." Other names include tropical croton, sand croton, and doveweed. Its seeds, located in a capsule, are plentiful, and numerous bird species eat them, especially doves. The flowers are a source of nectar for insects, and like goatweed, vente conmigo is a host plant for the goatweed leafwing butterfly. The plant also provides cover for small mammals and birds,[56] and deer browse vente conmigo.[57] This species ranges from South and Central America through Mexico and much of the United States.[58]

Threeseed mercury, *Acalypha gracilens,* is a low C-value annual native forb with a capsular fruit. It is able to thrive in dry to moist sites. Its native range in the United States is the southern Midwest and the East.[59] The seeds are eaten by birds, including quail, and deer browse the leaves.[60]

FIG. 78. Threeseed mercury, *Acalypha gracilens.*

FAMILY HYPERICACEAE (ALTERNATELY INCLUDED IN CLUSIACEAE): ST. JOHN'S WORT

This family is a cosmopolitan family of plants with nearly 700 species. They may be annual or perennial and they exist as herbaceous, shrub, and tree species.

FIG. 79. The yellow flower of St. Andrew's cross has four petals in the shape of a cross.

St. Andrew's cross, *Hypericum hypericoides,* is a small perennial shrub that has yellow flowers with four petals forming a cross. It prefers dry upland woodlands with acid soil. Its range extends through Central America, the Caribbean, Mexico, the southern Midwest, and the eastern United States.[61] Birds and mammals eat the seeds and foliage, and the flowers provide nectar and pollen to bees, flies, butterflies, and other insects.[62] Dwarf St. John's wort, *Hypericum mutilum,* has also been found on Wafer Creek Ranch, along with a few other varieties.[63]

FAMILY RUTACEAE: CITRUS

The citrus family is a large family that includes herbaceous plants, shrubs, and trees. They are mostly native to the tropical zones of the world and provide the well-known foods of the citrus family, such as limes, oranges, lemons, and grapefruits. Within the family there are more than 150 genera and around 1,600 species. On Wafer Creek Ranch, there may be only one member of the citrus family, *Ptelea trifoliata.*

Wafer ash (common hoptree), *Ptelea trifoliata,* is a deciduous perennial shrub or small tree of the citrus family that has three large leaflets. Birds eat the seeds, which are encased within a wafer-like samara, and the flowers provide nectar and pollen for hummingbirds, bees, flies, butterflies, and other insects. The plant is host to several insect larvae, including leafhopper larvae and the larvae of both the eastern tiger swallowtail butterfly and the giant swallowtail butterfly—the largest butterfly species in North America.[64]

Wafer ash grows in woodland sites and tolerates both moist and dry, rocky soils in full sun or partial shade. The range of wafer ash encompasses much of Mexico, the American West, and the Midwestern and eastern United States. The host plants for the giant swallowtail butterfly are members of the citrus family. Because wafer ash is likely the only member of the family extant on Wafer Creek Ranch, the butterflies are entirely dependent on the plant for egg laying and larval development. The caterpillar of the giant swallowtail is an excellent example of caterpillar deception, as the large hoodlike head and its facial eyes are fake. The true head of the animal is tucked under the hood, which is the fake head.

FIG. 80. *Left:* Wafer ash, *Ptelea trifoliata.*

FIG. 81. *Below left:* Caterpillar of the giant swallowtail butterfly. The large hoodlike head and beautiful frontal eyes are fake.

FIG. 82. *Below right:* Giant swallowtail butterfly—the largest butterfly species in North America.

FAMILY MELASTOMATACEAE: MEADOW BEAUTY

FIG. 83. Meadow beauty, *Rhexia mariana*. This meadow beauty has a hemipteran (of the order of true bugs) on its flower. Multiple species of bugs are pollinators. Insect identification thanks to entomologist Natalie Clay, Louisiana Tech University.

The meadow beauty family has more than 150 genera and up to about 3,000 species, which include herbs, shrubs, and trees, mostly inhabiting South and Central America, but the genus *Rhexia* is present in the United States and Cuba.[65]

Meadow beauty, *Rhexia mariana,* is a perennial forb that stands about one to two feet tall. Preferring damp, acid soils, its range in the United States is the southern Midwest and eastern United States.[66] The plant provides nectar and pollen for bees and other insects. Bumblebees practice buzz pollination, in which the bee's thoracic muscles vibrate the flower, inducing the flower's release of its pollen. Meadow beauty is spread by its seeds and rhizomes.[67]

FAMILY RANUNCULACEAE: BUTTERCUPS

A fairly large family, Ranunculaceae has about forty genera and nearly 2,000 species distributed worldwide. Most commonly, the seeds are located in an achene.

Devil's darning needles (woodbine or **virgin's bower**), *Clematis virginiana,* is a perennial vine that prefers sunny or partially shady wet or dry sites. The plant has striking plume-like achene aggregates, giving it a unique appearance. Only the female and perfect (dual-sexuality) flowers produce the achenes. These plants provide nectar and pollen to bees, wasps, flies, and other insects. It is also host plant for several moth species.[68] The leaves of *Clematis virginiana* are mostly trifoliate and have toothed (or notched) outer edges, which distinguishes it from the nonnative *Clematis terniflora*. Its range is the southern Midwest and eastern United States.[69]

FIG. 84. Devil's darning needles, *Clematis virginiana*. The "bad-hair guys" in the photo are achene aggregates.

FAMILY GENTIANACEAE: GENTIANS

The Gentian family is a cosmopolitan family with more than seventy-five genera and nearly 1,600 species. The plant members of the genus *Sabatia* are outstanding wildflowers of the family Gentianaceae.

FIG. 85. Rose gentian, *Sabatia* species.

Rose gentian. *Sabatia* is the genus of the rose gentians, of which there are about twenty species. This genus is native to central and eastern North America, including Nova Scotia, Central America, and the Caribbean. They occur as annual or perennial plants. The species on Wafer Creek Ranch might be rose pink, *Sabatia angularis,* an annual or biennial forb. Insects such as butterflies, including skipper butterflies, and bees gather nectar and pollen from the flowers, and rose pink is a host plant to a moth species.[70] It prefers partial shade in moist areas.

FAMILY ONAGRACEAE: EVENING PRIMROSE

This family has twenty-two genera and more than 600 species. The plants of the evening primrose family typically have brightly colored flowers with four sepals and petals. Representative plants of onagraceae occur worldwide.

FIG. 86. Beeblossom, *Oenothera (Gaura) linheimeri.*

FIG. 87. Common evening primrose, *Oenothera biennis.*

Beeblossom, *Oenothera (Gaura) lindheimeri,* is a rhizomatous, colony-forming perennial with range restricted to northeastern Mexico, Louisiana, and Texas.[71] It grows in moist to dry soil and in full sun to partial shade. Beeblossom provides nectar and pollen to bees, butterflies, and moths.[72] The flowers are eye-catching and appear asymmetrical, with their four petals situated on one side, usually pointing upward.

Common evening primrose, *Oenothera biennis,* is a large, two- to six-foot-tall weedy biennial forb. Invisible to humans, the flower has a "nectar guide," a pattern that can be seen by nectar-gathering insects such as moths, butterflies, and bees that see in ultraviolet light. Birds eat the seeds and mammals browse the leaves; hummingbirds gather nectar from the flowers. The plant is host to the primrose moth and white-lined sphinx moth. It also was a source of food and medicine for Native peoples.[73] Common evening primrose prefers moist soil in sunny locations. Its native range is most of North America and southern Canada.[74]

FAMILY CONVOLVULACEAE: MORNING GLORY (SWEET POTATO)

This family has about sixty genera and more than 1,600 species. It is composed mostly of vines but also some shrubs and trees. Some species, such as the sweet potato, are known for their tuberous roots.

Wild potato vine, *Ipomoea pandurata,* is a high C-value perennial vine with tuberous roots that are edible when roasted; they were utilized as a food source by Native people.[75] The plant provides nectar and pollen to hummingbirds, moths, butterflies, bees, and other insects, while some species of beetle feed on the leaves.[76] It is a host plant for the larvae of some beetle and moth species.[77] Wild potato vine prefers full sun or partially shady sites that have mesic to dry soils. The range of this species is the Midwest and eastern United States to Ontario.[78]

FIG. 88. Wild potato vine, *Ipomoea pandurata.*

Hairy clustervine, *Jacquemontia tamnifolia,* is a weedy and prolific scrambling and climbing vine up to fifteen feet long. An annual, its range is from South and Central America to Mexico, and from Texas eastward to South Carolina, being primarily centered in the coastal states.[79] Farther north, it becomes more scattered and local. The pollinated flowers of hairy clustervine form fuzzy, discoid clusters.

Tievine, *Ipomoea cordatotriloba,* is a usually aggressive, weedy perennial vine, sometimes having leaves that range from heart-shaped to being distinctly trilobed. The native range of tievine extends from South and Central America, Mexico, Texas, and the coastal states to North Carolina.[80] Able to tolerate dry sites, it also can grow in damp zones, where it becomes quite weedy. The flowers attract moths and butterflies.[81] As the family name morning glory suggests, the blooms are striking in the early morning, but die back after a little warm sunshine, which is what is happening to the flowers in figure 90.

FIG. 89. Hairy clustervine, *Jacquemontia tamnifolia.*

FIG. 90. Tievine, *Ipomoea cordatotriloba.* Notice the flowers beginning to wilt in the sunlight.

FAMILY SOLANACEAE: NIGHTSHADES

This family contains nearly 100 genera. Many species contain highly toxic alkaloids, but we are most familiar with tobacco and those species that are important and popular cuisine, such as tomatoes, tomatillos, eggplant, potatoes, and chili peppers. The Solanaceae family is distributed worldwide but most species occur in tropical America, where most of the foods of the family originated, only later to become popular around the world.

FIG. 91. Carolina horsenettle, *Solanum carolinense.*

Carolina horsenettle, *Solanum carolinense,* is a perennial forb whose flower and fruit resemble those of tomatoes. However, horsenettle is toxic. It is a weedy low C-value forb that spreads by seed and underground rhizomes. The flower nectar and pollen is fed on by insects, including bumblebees that utilize buzz pollination, and it is a host plant for certain moth species. Beetles also eat the foliage, and birds and skunks eat the fruit and seeds. The plant's present range is throughout much of North America, but mainly in the east, including eastern Canada.[82] There are a few other native members of this family on Wafer Creek Ranch, such as *Solanum ptychanthum* (eastern black nightshade) and *Physalis pubescens* (groundcherry).

FAMILY CAMPANULACEAE: BLUEBELLS/BELLFLOWERS

The bluebell family contains about eighty-four genera and about 2,400 species of herbaceous plants, shrubs, and occasionally small trees. It's a cosmopolitan family with members occurring mostly in temperate zones and in cool, mountainous tropical zones.[83] Hawaii has more than one hundred endemic members of Campanulaceae.[84] There are several members of the *Lobelia* genus on Wafer Creek Ranch, including pale lobelia, the striking cardinal flower, and downy lobelia. These flowers have the typical enlarged three-lobed lower lip found in many *Lobelia.*

FIG. 92. Pale lobelia, *Lobelia appendiculata.*   FIG. 93. Downy lobelia, *Lobelia puberula.*

Pale lobelia, *Lobelia appendiculata,* has a range primarily centered in Louisiana, Arkansas, and Texas, but it extends somewhat slightly to more isolated locations elsewhere in the southern Midwest and southeastern United States.[85] Pale lobelia is an annual to biennial forb that, on Wafer Creek Ranch, blooms primarily in the spring and prefers open sunny locations.[86] The flowers provide nectar and pollen to insects.

Downy lobelia, *Lobelia puberula,* is a perennial forb member of the bluebell family that blooms in late summer and fall. It prefers full sun to partial shade and moist to relatively dryer (mesic) sites. Downy lobelia is an excellent nectar and pollen provider to hummingbirds, bees, butterflies, flies, wasps, and other insects.[87] Deer browse the plants. The native range of downy lobelia is the southern Midwest and eastern United States.[88]

Cardinal flower, *Lobelia cardinalis,* is a perennial forb that grows in swamps, along stream sides and pond edges. Though not a typical grassland species, cardinal flower does grow in woodland uplands along natural ditches and draws, where the specimen in figure 94 was found. The flowers provide nec-

tar to hummingbirds, which are their principal pollinators.[89] The range of cardinal flower is from Colombia through Central America, Mexico, and into the western, Midwestern, and eastern United States to Canada.[90]

FIG. 94. *Above:* Cardinal flower, *Lobelia cardinalis.* This little specimen was growing in an upland site on WCR. It well demonstrates the trilobed lower flower lip seen in many plants of the *Lobelia* genus.

FIG. 95. *Right:* Clasping Venus' looking-glass, *Triodanis perfoliata.*

Clasping Venus' looking-glass, *Triodanis perfoliata,* is a largely unbranching native annual forb member of the Campanulaceae family. Its native range encompasses most of the western hemisphere, from Argentina to Canada, and it is present throughout the United States.[91] The plant blooms in spring, with a few stragglers in early summer. The leaves of the plant clasp the stem, meaning the leaves' attachments reach at least partially around the stem. Venus' looking-glass prefers full sun in mesic to dry sites. Deer and rabbits browse the plants and the flowers provide pollen and nectar to bees, butterflies, and other insects.[92]

FAMILY SCROPHULARIACEAE: SNAPDRAGONS (FIGWORTS)

Where have all the dragons gone?
Scientists took 'em, every one!

Not exactly. But the snapdragon family has fairly recently been brought to its knees by the inconvenient truth of DNA sequencing of its chloroplast gene, causing the family to lose a number of its genera to other plant families, including the plantain and broomrape families.[93]

The plantain family has recently been placed under the order *Lamiales.* Nodding penstemon and Texas toadflax are orphan species previously designated as members of the snapdragon family.

Nodding penstemon (nodding beardtongue), *Penstemon laxiflorus,* has a range centered in Texas, Louisiana, southern Oklahoma, and southern Arkansas, becoming more dispersed and local in the eastern coastal states, to Georgia and Florida.[94] It is a perennial forb that blooms in the spring and early summer and thrives in partially shady, dry woodland sites. The plant's leaves clasp the stem. The flowers provide nectar and pollen to hummingbirds, bees, and other insects.[95]

Texas toadflax, *Nuttallanthus texanus,* is a slender upright species with a height of up to about two feet or more. It is a common annual spring forb on Wafer Creek Ranch and has a native range that takes in the southern and western United States from Mexico to Canada.[96] Texas toadflax is a nectar and pollen source for butterflies and other pollinators and a host plant for the common buckeye butterfly.[97]

FIG. 96. Nodding penstemon, *Penstemon laxiflorus.*

FIG. 97. Texas toadflax, *Nuttallanthus texanus.*

This family consists primarily of parasitic and hemiparasitic plants. It has about ninety genera and more than 2,000 species. Many of the genera were previously included in the snapdragon family.[98]

Beach false foxglove, *Agalinis fasciculata*, is a native annual forb of the southern Midwest and eastern United States.[99] It is partially parasitic (hemiparasitic), meaning that although the plant contains chlorophyll, its roots connect to neighboring plant species, usually grasses, to steal their nutrients (primarily sugar). Beach false foxglove blooms in summer and fall. Its flowers provide nectar and pollen to insects and hummingbirds, and like Texas toadflax, it is a host plant for the common buckeye butterfly.[100]

FIG. 98. *Above:* Beach false foxglove, *Agalinis fasciculata.*

FIG. 99. *Above right:* Common buckeye caterpillar on beach false foxglove (one of its host plants).

FIG. 100. *Below right:* Common buckeye butterfly on late boneset.

FAMILY POLYGALACEAE: MILKWORTS

The milkwort family has a worldwide distribution, with nearly 900 species of herbaceous plants, shrubs, and trees. Over half of the species are in one genus, *Polygala.*

Purple milkwort, *Polygala polygama,* is a small biennial herbaceous plant that has a native range extending from the southern Midwest throughout the eastern United States to eastern Canada.[101] Purple milkwort grows in full sun or in dry, partially shaded woodlands, and it blooms in spring and early summer on Wafer Creek Ranch.[102] The flowers provide nectar and pollen to bees, flies, butterflies, and other insects, and deer browse the plants.[103]

FIG. 101. Purple milkwort, *Polygala polygama.*

FAMILY ORCHIDACEAE: ORCHIDS

The largest flowering plant family in the world, Orchidaceae likely has more than 27,000 known species and more than 750 known genera, all of which are perennials, often rhizomatous or with corms or tubers. Orchids are monocots, usually having simple leaves with parallel veins, but there are exceptions. The lower medial petal of the flower often forms a lip structure, which serves as a platform for pollinators. Orchids have a worldwide distribution but most of the family's diversity is in the tropics, where the majority of the plants exist as epiphytes anchored to trees or shrubs. Virtually all orchids have at least some mycorrhizal associations during their lifetimes. There are four species of orchid identified on Wafer Creek Ranch; only two, however, are presented here.

Ladies' tresses orchids belong to *Spiranthes,* a cosmopolitan genus with a spirally arranged inflorescence primarily pollinated by bumblebees.[104] One or more species can be found throughout the United States and Canada, and

there are several species of ladies' tresses orchids known in Louisiana. Most species prefer sunny locations. Ladies' tresses are perennial monocot forbs that may bloom from June to November.

Cranefly orchid, *Tipularia discolor,* is a delicate but striking little orchid. The flower comes up in midsummer and early fall, but by that time the leaf (each plant has one leaf) will have died away (during the preceding late spring), having flourished over the winter months. Nonetheless, the plants are perennial, and the leaves come up again later in the fall and winter. The elongate leaves are rather broad, with green upper surfaces, but they have purple

undersides, which is an excellent field mark. A plant of the woodland, it is the only species of the *Tipularia* genus in North America. The plants are propagated both by seeds and by the plant's corms, which are edible. Cranefly orchid is pollinated by noctuid moths. As is the case with many orchids, the flower has pollinia, specialized structures containing pollen. When a moth comes for the nectar, the pollinia attach to one of its compound eyes so that the moth can transfer the pollen onto the next cranefly flower for pollination.[105] The plant's range is the southern Midwest and eastern United States.[106] As with the rest of the members of the orchid family, the cranefly orchid has a mycorrhizal relationship and thereby tends to grow where there is rotting wood in moist soil.

FAMILY ERICACEAE: HEATH

Ericaceae is a large family of about 120 genera and around 4,000 species. This is the family of cranberries, huckleberries, blueberries, and rhododendrons. We recall that huckleberries and blueberries are important members of the WCR shortleaf pine-oak-hickory woodland midstory. Ericaceae has a worldwide distribution, and examples can be found from the cold latitudes to tropical zones. Many members utilize mycorrhizal fungi for assistance in nutrient capture, and many examples of this family are evergreen. The herbaceous plant I picked for this work is a truly unusual member of the Heath family, as you will see.

Indian pipe, *Monotropa uniflora,* may look like a fungus, but it is actually a perennial herbaceous flowering plant of the Heath family and it serves as a good example of what might be called "deviant underworld activities." It is often white or pinkish-white and lacks chlorophyll; thus, the plant is deprived of the ability to generate sugar from sunlight, the energy source of plants with green leaves. The fascinating way in which Indian pipe gets its sugar is through its relationship with a mycorrhizal fungus, which in turn taps into the sugar source of the roots of plants that do utilize the chlorophyll–sunlight reaction.

FIG. 104. Indian pipe, *Monotropa uniflora.*

In this case, the plant with green leaves (a chlorophyllic plant) has a symbiotic relationship with the mycorrhizal fungus in that it provides the fungus with sugar and in turn receives soil nutrients (such as nitrogen, phosphate, iron, and water) from the fungus. But here, the Indian pipe steps in and robs the sugar from the fungus. In short, Indian pipe is parasitic to a plant host with green leaves, such as a tree, but it uses a mycorrhizal fungus as the middleman by stealing the sugar that the fungus had gained by fair trade. (Obviously, it could be argued that Indian pipe is parasitic to *both* the photosynthetic plant *and* the fungus.)[107]

Though Indian pipe is a perennial, it often sprouts only in certain years when the conditions are right for the plant. The flower has a very strong, sweet odor and attracts insects. A species of thrips feeds on the flowers and bumblebees are pollinators for the plant. Bears are known to eat the plants and roots.[108] Because Indian pipe doesn't utilize sunlight, it can thrive in a dark, shady forest. The plant can be found in the temperate regions of Asia and North America as well as northern South America.[109]

FAMILY PASSIFLORACEAE: PASSION FLOWERS

FIG. 105. Purple passion flower, *Passiflora incarnata.*

Passion flowers (passion vines) are members of the passifloraceae family and are quite common on Wafer Creek Ranch, where two species have been identified: purple passion flower, *Passiflora incarnata,* and yellow passion flower, *Passiflora lutea.* Both species are vines and are host plants for the Gulf fritillary and variegated fritillary butterflies and several other butterfly and moth species. Additionally, the flowers are nectar and pollen sources for bees and other insects, as well as for hummingbirds. The passion fruit is eaten by birds.[110] The purple passion flower vines are particularly robust, large and hardy, and they are fast growers over the warm months of the year. The fruit (passion fruit or maypop) is edible and is even cultivated as a food. The name maypop comes from the notion that if you step on the fruit it indeed may pop. The native range of both species are the southern Midwest and eastern North America.[111]

FIG. 106. Passion fruit of the purple passion flower, *Passiflora incarnata.*

FIG. 107. Yellow passion flower, *Passiflora lutea.*

FIG. 108. Gulf fritillary butterfly gathering nectar from a hairy cluster vine blossom. Passion vines of genus *Passiflora* are the host plants for this butterfly.

FIG. 109. The variegated fritillary butterfly also uses passion vines as a host plant.

FAMILY ASTERACEAE: SUNFLOWERS

The second-largest flowering plant family on Earth, after the orchid family, is Asteraceae, the sunflowers. These plants play a valuable role in all grassland ecosystems, including those of woodlands. The flowers of members of this family usually demonstrate a central disk with surrounding "petals." But the disk is packed with numerous tiny individual flowers, or disk flowers, and the petals are actually corollas of individual flowers themselves, called ray flowers. For this reason, the members of the sunflower family are called composites. Many species of this family are notorious for the speciation difficulties they present to botanists and sunflower enthusiasts. Lady Bird Johnson and others have called these difficult species "DYCs," for "damn yellow composites."[112] An interesting corollary is the birders' term used for difficult-to-identify small brown birds that sometimes get passed over as "LBJs," "little brown jobs."

Woolly ragwort, *Packera tomentosa,* is an early spring blooming species and rapid grower as it unexpectedly sprouts upward, often against an otherwise brown and largely dormant-appearing landscape. Woolly ragwort is a southerner primarily residing in the coastal plain states from East Texas and south-

FIG. 110. Woolly ragwort, *Packera tomentosa*. Notice the spade-shaped leaves at the base of the plant.

east Oklahoma eastward to the southern Atlantic states.[113] The plant is a perennial with spade-shaped leaves largely restricted to ground level. The few leaves arising from its stem are elongated and pointed, with leaf margins that are serrated. Woolly ragwort is often grayish, due to the plant's hairiness (tomentose). Butterweed, *Packera glabella,* is an annual and early spring lookalike that can be distinguished from woolly ragwort by its rounded leaflets with distinctly toothy margins, and its leaves are cauline—meaning the leaves extend from the stem along its length.

FIG. 111. Blackeyed Susan, *Rudbeckia hirta.*

Blackeyed Susan, *Rudbeckia hirta,* is a showy, well-known sunflower with a range extending throughout most of North America.[114] An early summer–blooming annual to short-lived perennial, it serves as host plant for bordered patch and gorgone checkerspot butterflies and it provides nectar and pollen for numerous insects. Typical of so many sunflowers, it is a seed source for birds.[115]

Rough coneflower, *Rudbeckia grandiflora,* is a high C-value grassland perennial sunflower sometimes reaching up to five feet and having a large, cone-shaped flower head. It has an interesting native range as it's located almost exclusively on the west side of the Mississippi River, yet centered in Louisiana, Arkansas, East Texas, Oklahoma, and only a few scattered counties in Missouri and Kansas, where it's rare.[116] The stems and leaves have a rather rough feel due to their hairy surfaces; hence the plant's common name. Bees, bugs, beetles, and butterflies gather the nectar and pollen.[117] Deer browse the leaves and stems of rough coneflower, and birds such as quail and doves eat its seed.[118]

FIG. 112. Rough coneflower, *Rudbeckia grandifolia.* Wild bergamot (purple) in background.

Camphorweed, *Pluchea camphorata,* is a fairly large native annual with large clusters of flowers that attract insects. *Pluchea* gives off a pungent, stinky-socks type of odor, especially when the large leaves are crushed. Often enough, some botanist or plant enthusiast will shout out, "Hey! Who cut a pluchea?!" Its native range extends across the southern Midwest and southeastern North America.[119]

FIG. 113. Camphorweed, *Pluchea camphorata.*

FIG. 114. The "other" camphorweed, *Heterotheca subaxillaris.*

Camphorweed, *Heterotheca subaxillaris,* might be considered the "other" camphorweed of WCR. However, its crushed leaves emit an odor that truly smells like camphor, unlike the stinky-socks odor of *Pluchea camphorata. Heterotheca subaxillaris* is a native aromatic annual to short-lived perennial with clasping leaves. *Heterotheca* grows to five or more feet tall. Host plants to larval forms of flies and moths, the plants are also a nectar and pollen source for insects, and the seeds attract birds, including wild turkeys.[120] The plant's range encompasses southern North America from the Pacific to the Atlantic, as well as Mexico and Belize.[121]

Crownbeards, *Verbesinas,* are fairly common on Wafer Creek Ranch, where at least two species of this large genus exist. They are rhizomatous perennials and excellent nectar and pollen sources for insects. *Verbesina helianthoides,* yellow crownbeard, is host plant for the silvery checkerspot butterfly and the gold moth.[122] *Verbesina virginica,* white crownbeard, has large white flower clusters that attract hordes of bees, hoverflies, wasps, butterflies, and hummingbirds. Yellow crownbeard and white crownbeard are both four- to six-foot-tall erect species that stand out in the groundcover, and both have ranges encompassing the southern Midwest and eastern United States.[123]

FIG. 115. White crownbeard, *Verbesina virginica.* Look hard and you'll see two or three bumblebees on this plant.

FIG. 116. Yellow crownbeard, *Verbesina helianthoides.*

FIG. 117. Ice ribbons of frost plants (crownbeards) are common in subfreezing weather.

The verbesinas are also called wingstems, because of the leafy ridges, or wings, that run the length of the stems, and frost plants, because interesting ice ribbons exude from the stem bases in subfreezing weather.

Wild lettuce, *Lactuca* species, is the genus of the sunflower family making up the lettuces, of which there are about fifty or more species worldwide. The genus includes the common garden lettuces. Often the flowers are yellow, but the little wild lettuce in figure 118 has purple flowers. Lettuces with white or blue flowers also exist.

A diverse group, they may exist as perennials, annuals, biennials, or shrubs. *Lactuca canadensis* (Canada lettuce) is considered a native in central North America. It is a tall, common ditch weed along unmowed rights-of-ways. Canada lettuce has yellow flowers. The lettuces typically have noticeably deeply lobed leaves.

FIG. 118. Wild lettuce, *Lactuca floridana.* Species identification by Larry Allain.

FIG. 119. The leaves of the *Lactuca* in this photo demonstrate the prominent lobes seen in many members of the genus.

FIG. 120. Bushy goldentop, *Euthamia leptocephala*.

Bushy goldentop, *Euthamia leptocephala*, has a native range somewhat restricted to Louisiana, Texas, Arkansas, and Mississippi but with some sparse and scattered spillover to adjacent states.[124] The leaves of bushy goldentop are long, narrow, and pointed, reminiscent of those of sweet goldenrod. It is a rhizomatous perennial forb forming colonies and having flowers that provide nectar and pollen to bees and other insects.[125]

Roundleaf thoroughwort, *Eupatorium rotundifolium*, is a native perennial, up to three feet tall, of a genus that contains some very weedy plants. Weedy low C-value species usually tend to be common throughout a site, but sometimes an interesting lesser common plant may stand out such that even if one cannot identify it, that species will catch your eye and arouse your curiosity. Such is case with roundleaf thoroughwort, a fairly high C-value forb and an excellent nectar and pollen provider for insects, especially bees.[126] Its seeds are eaten by birds. The plant's range is the southern Midwest and much of eastern North America.[127] As its name implies, this thoroughwort has rounded leaves.

Members of the genus *Eupatorium* are often called bonesets or thoroughworts. One exception on WCR is the native but frequently invasive *Eupatorium capillifolium,* variously called cypress weed, Yankee weed, or dog fennel. It is a target plant in my herbicide work as it can, unless existing only in small numbers, impede the progress of the restoration.

FIG. 121. Roundleaf thoroughwort, *Eupatorium rotundifolium.*

White boneset, *Eupatorium album,* is a high C-value grassland perennial of open pinelands. It grows to only about three feet tall, and its range takes in the southern midstates (the states hugging the Mississippi River, up to Minnesota) and northeastward to New York.[128] The plant's leaves are for the most part opposite, with toothy margins, and due to their hairiness, the stems appear grayish. White boneset is imperiled or extirpated in several northeastern states. As it is with all the bonesets on WCR, it should serve as a good species for pollinators.

FIG. 122. White boneset, *Eupatorium album.*

FIG. 123. Common boneset, *Eupatorium perfoliatum.* Notice how the stem appears to perforate the fused leaves.

Common boneset, *Eupatorium perfoliatum,* is a rhizomatous perennial with hairy stems. It has interesting opposite leaves that clasp around the stem and fuse together, giving the appearance of the stem having perforated a single bow-shaped leaf. The flower's nectar and pollen attracts bees, flies, wasps, butterflies, and beetles. It serves as host plant for a variety of moth species: clymene, lined ruby tiger, Burdock borer, blackberry looper, three-lined flower, and geometrid.[129] Common boneset's native range is the Midwest and throughout the eastern states and much of Canada.[130]

FIG. 124. Late boneset, *Eupatorium serotinum.*

Late boneset (late thoroughwort), *Eupatorium serotinum,* is a rhizomatous perennial forb that can reach five to seven feet tall. It blooms in the fall and thrives in sunny, damp to dry upland sites. Late boneset depends on insects for its pollination and propagation, and it provides nectar and pollen to bees, butterflies, flies, pollen-eating beetles, and other insects.[131] The plant is host to several moth species and the seeds are eaten by birds.[132] Late boneset is common in the Midwest and eastern United States.[133] Unlike roundleaf thoroughwort, late boneset has long, lance-like leaves with serrated margins.

Late boneset is yet another example of a weedy, low C-value wildflower that plays a big role in the ecosystem because of its support of insect diversity and its service as a food source for birds.

Late purple aster (spreading aster), *Symphyotrichum patens,* is a high C-value perennial forb with leaves clasping the stem. It's also called spreading aster because the branches spread out widely from the main plant stem, often having a single flower at the end of a branch.[134] Fall bloomers, late purple

FIG. 125. Late purple aster, *Symphyotrichum patens.* Notice how the leaves clasp the stems. Photo credit: Larry Allain, US Geological Survey.

FIG. 126. Late purple aster, *Symphyotrichum patens.* Notice how the branches of this specimen extend outward at almost right angles to the main stem, often with a single flower located at the end of the branch. "Spreading aster" is a good name for this plant.

asters grow well in partially shaded woodland settings, and they are important in providing nectar and pollen for insects such as bees and butterflies.[135] Late purple aster's native range is the southern Midwest and eastern United States.[136]

The **blazing stars** of genus *Liatris* contain a large number of species that are some of the most spectacular bloomers in grassland ecosystems. Host plants to flower moths, the blazing stars rank near the top of the list as nectar and pollen sources for insects and hummingbirds.[137] The species of this genus are native to North America from southern Canada to northern Mexico.[138] Blazing stars are generally high C-value perennials with underground bulblike root structures called corms. Among the numerous species, the three presently known to exist on Wafer Creek Ranch are prairie blazing star, tall blazing star, and elegant blazing star.

FIG. 127. Prairie blazing stars visited by a pair of common buckeye butterflies.

Prairie blazing star, *Liatris pycnostachya,* is native primarily to the Midwestern states.[139] It is a robust and large species and an important food source for nectar- and pollen-seeking insects and hummingbirds.[140] Birds eat the seeds, and the leaves and stems are consumed by browsers such as deer and rabbits.[141]

FIG. 128. Tall blazing
star, *Liatris aspera.*

Tall blazing star (rough blazing star), *Liatris aspera,* easily reaches six feet tall. Its native range encompasses the Midwest and eastern North America.[142] Its faunal associations are similar to those of prairie blazing star.

FIG. 129. Elegant blazing star, *Liatris elegans*. Notice the scattered white flowers with the background of violet-purple. Of all the Wafer Creek Ranch wildflowers, this one's a razzla-dazzla!

Elegant blazing star, *Liatris elegans,* is a Deep South plant of the southern Midwest and coastal plain states.[143] It blooms later than the preceding two species, usually in mid-September to early November. Tall blazing star and prairie blazing star bloom in July through August and usually are bloomed out by the time the elegant blazing star blossoms emerge. Elegant blazing star is well named and truly elegant. The light violet-purple inflorescences have a few scattered white blossoms, giving them a uniquely striking appearance. It can grow to four feet and is my personal favorite of the bunch, a real beauty, with faunal associations similar to the two preceding species.

Mistflower, *Conoclinium coelestinum,* is a common fall blooming member of the composites. Sometimes called wild ageratum, it is a North

American low C-value perennial with a range encompassing the southern Midwest and extending throughout the eastern states.[144] Birds eat mistflower seeds in the fall and winter and the flowers are an excellent source of nectar and pollen for insects such as bees and butterflies. The plant also serves as host to several moth species.[145] Mistflower is a colony-growing plant due to its highly rhizomatous root system.[146]

Rice button aster, *Symphyotrichum dumosum*, is a fall blooming perennial of the southern Midwest and eastern North America, and it's an important food source for many animals including nectar- and pollen-seeking insects (bees, butterflies, flies, wasps, and others).[147] Several species of insect, such as beetles, grasshoppers, hemipterans (true bugs), and caterpillars of moths and butterflies eat the plants' leaves. Birds eat the seeds, and deer and rabbits eat the leaves and stems.[148] The plant has rhizomatous roots, and like mistflower, rice button aster is a low C-value forb. But remember, though a species may have a

FIG. 130. Mistflower, *Conoclinium coelestinum* (purple flowers), and rice button aster *Symphyotrichum dumosum* (white flowers).

low C-value, this doesn't mean that it's not of great value to the ecosystem. It simply means the plant can easily invade sites of soil disturbance—which in this case seems like a good thing, considering the great service to fauna rice button aster and mistflower provide.

White snakeroot, *Ageratina altissima,* is a rhizomatous perennial forb that prefers partial shade. The flowers provide nectar and pollen to bees, butterflies, flies, and moths and the plant serves as host to caterpillars of several moth species.[149]

White snakeroot has striking snow white flowers, but it contains tremetol, which is deadly to livestock and humans. There have been numerous fatalities among humans who have eaten the plant or drunk the milk from cows that have grazed on white snakeroot. The condition is called "milk sickness," to which the death of Abraham Lincoln's mother, Nancy, is attributed.[150] Anna Bixby is credited with discovering that the plant's toxin was the cause of the deadly milk sickness, but reportedly only after it was first explained to her

FIG. 131. White snakeroot, *Ageratina altissima.*

by a Shawnee woman whose name is now lost to history.[151] (One has to wonder how many other important discoveries were handed over to us from aboriginal peoples who never got the credit they deserve.)

Early settlers erroneously believed that the roots of white snakeroot would serve as treatment for snakebite; hence its common name. However, if the victim survived the snake's venom (and the victim probably would have), the poisonous root antidote itself might have taken the poor snakebite victim out. The golden rule of patient care is "First, do no harm"!

The range of white snakeroot is the Midwestern and eastern United States and much of Canada.[152]

Oldfield aster (frost aster), *Symphyotrichum pilosum,* is an upright perennial aster with hairy stems and leaves; hence its species name, *pilosum.* Its native range is the Midwest and eastern North America to Canada.[153] It blooms on WCR in the fall and prefers well-drained sites in full sun. Bees, including bumblebees, as well as flies, butterflies, and moths gather nectar and pollen from its flowers. Oldfield aster serves as a host plant for the larvae of midges, leafhoppers, some moth species, grasshoppers, walking sticks, and pearl crescent butterflies. Turkeys, sparrows, and mice eat the seeds. Deer and rabbits browse the foliage.[154]

FIG. 132. Oldfield aster, *Symphyotrichum pilosum.* Notice the hairy stems and leaves of this aster.

Narrowleaf sunflower, *Helianthus angustifolius,* is a spectacular perennial fall sunflower growing up to ten feet tall. It has long, narrow scratchy (scabrous) leaves and bright glow-yellow flowers that provide nectar and pollen

FIG. 133. Narrowleaf sunflower, *Helianthus angustifolius.*

FIG. 134. *Below:* Shown here are the long, thin leaves of narrowleaf sunflower. They feel scratchy, like sandpaper.

to insects and serve as natural bird feeders in the late fall and early winter. Small mammals eat the seeds, and the plants are host to the silvery checkerspot butterfly.[155] Narrowleaf sunflower prefers full sun in both damp lowland and dry upland habitats. The range of narrowleaf sunflower encompasses the southern Midwest and the eastern United States.[156]

Rough woodland sunflower, *Helianthus divaricatus,* is a perennial forb composite that thrives in the partial shade of woodlands as well as in full sun. It is propagated both by the plant's rhizomes and by seeds, and it blooms in summer and fall.[157] The flowers provide nectar and pollen for a large list of insects, and the plant is host for the silvery checkerspot, gorgone checkerspot, painted lady butterflies, and several species of moth. Additionally, birds and mammals eat the seeds.[158] The leaves of rough woodland sunflower are scratchy; hence the word "rough" in the name. The plant's native range is the Midwest and eastern North America.[159] There are only a few specimens of this sunflower on Wafer Creek Ranch and they represent a new species for Lincoln Parish.

FIG. 135. Rough woodland sunflower, *Helianthus divaricatus.*

FIG. 136. Soft golden-aster, *Chrysopsis pilosa.*

Soft goldenaster, *Chrysopsis pilosa,* is a common annual of dry upland sites primarily in the southern Midwest.[160] It is a nectar and pollen source for insects as well as an example of one of those sunflower members that provide us with the familiar "fuzz balls of fall," the plants' seed heads.

FIG. 137. Hairy fleabane, *Erigeron pulchellus.*

Hairy fleabane (Robin's plantain), *Erigeron pulchellus,* is a spring perennial rhizomatous forb having a native range extending from the Midwest through most of the eastern United States.[161] Its stems and leaves are noticeably hairy. It is a nectar and pollen source for bees, flies, and butterflies, and the plant is host to several moth species. Deer and rabbits eat the foliage, and the seeds are a food source for mice and other small rodents.[162]

Pussytoes, *Antennaria plantaginifolia,* is a cool season spring forb that grows well in the acidic, poor soils of the partially shaded woodlands of Wafer Creek Ranch. Like hairy fleabane, it is a perennial that, because of its stoloniferous propagation, grows in colonies. The leaves and stems are hairy, giving the plants a grayish appearance, and the stems bear clusters of flowers that may be white or pinkish-white. The flowers attract bees and flies, and the plants are host to several moth species as well as the painted lady and American lady butterflies.[163] Birds eat the seeds and deer and rabbits browse the foliage.[164] The plant's range is the Midwest and eastern United States.[165]

FIG. 138. Pussytoes, *Antennaria plantaginifolia,* a spring ephemeral.

Texas ironweed, *Vernonia texana,* has a native range centered in the southern Midwest, primarily Louisiana, Texas, Oklahoma, and Arkansas, and in a few counties of southern Mississippi.[166] A high C-value upright-growing perennial forb, Texas ironweed can be identified by its flowers as well as by the thin, elongate, scabrous leaves that strongly resemble those of narrowleaf sunflower. The flowers are popular with nectar- and pollen-foraging insects.[167]

FIG. 139. Texas ironweed, *Vernonia texana.*

Bidens sunflower (beggarticks), *Bidens aristosa,* is a large, bushy common forb sunflower with fruits that are dry achenes. The achenes have small barbs that stick to those who tread within their location. Bidens is a low C-value plant that may stand five feet or more in height and typically has many large yellow flowers. The plant is an annual to biennial and the flowers resemble

FIG. 140. *Below:* Bidens sunflower, *Bidens aristosa.*

FIG. 141. *Right:* Carolina elephant's foot, *Elephantopus carolinianus.* The leaves grow from the main stem along its length (cauline growth).

those of narrowleaf sunflower, but Bidens has compound leaves with toothed margins, quite unlike the thin, scratchy leaves of narrowleaf sunflower. Bidens prefers full sun in damp soil but can tolerate dryer sites. Due to its many flowers, it is an excellent nectar and pollen provider for bees, butterflies, flies, wasps, and other insects, and birds eat the seeds. It is host plant to several moth species, and leaf beetles eat the leaves. Rabbits also eat the leaves, and small rodents eat the seed.[168] The range of Bidens is primarily centered in the Midwest but it also extends to the eastern states and southern Canada.[169]

Carolina elephant's foot, *Elephantopus carolinianus,* is a perennial forb that blooms in summer and fall. It's a large plant that grows to about four feet tall and two to three feet wide, having broad alternate leaves extending from the main stem (or stalk) for a considerable distance along its length. As the stem gains height, it branches into compound inflorescences with flower stalks and their green, leafy bracts supporting the flowers. Carolina elephant's foot can sometimes have broad basal leaves, as is seen with common elephant's foot. The plant's range is the southern Midwest and eastern United States.[170] The flowers provide nectar and pollen to pollinators such as butterflies, and to other insects. Deer browse the plants and birds eat the seeds.[171]

Common elephant's foot, *Elephantopus tomentosus,* is a perennial forb that prefers dry, well-drained soil in full to partial sun. The leaves grow around the stalk of the plant in a basal location, flat on the ground, and usually do not grow along the stalk above ground level. The flower stalks, however, do have green leafy bracts supporting the flowers. The plant's range is Mexico, the southern Midwest, and the southeastern coastal plain in the United States.[172] The flowers of common elephant's foot provide nectar and pollen for bees, butterflies, and other insects.[173] Birds eat the seeds and deer browse the plant.

FIG. 142. Common elephant's foot, *Elephantopus tomentosus.* Notice the flat basal leaves on the ground and the green, leafy flower bracts supporting the purple flowers.

Rabbit tobacco, *Pseudognaphalium obtusifolium* and *P. helleri,* are annual to biennial forb members of the sunflower family. *P. obtusifolium*'s range is the Midwest, the eastern United States, and eastern Canada, but the less common *P. helleri,* also identified on WCR, has a range shifted farther eastward.[174] The plants, especially *P. obtusifolium,* have a prominent grayish-blue appearance due to their soft hairs. The flowers are creamy white and they, along with the leaves and bracts, have a characteristic somewhat sweet odor—it's one of my favorite scents in nature, and it's present practically year-round, as it's just as striking in dried specimens of winter. Rabbit tobacco is propagated by seed, and the plant thrives in dry, sunny to partially shady locations. Wasps, flies, bees, butterflies, and other insects gather nectar and pollen from the flowers, and deer and turkey eat the leaves.[175] Rabbit tobacco is larval host plant for the American lady butterfly.[176] It was used by several Native tribes for its medicinal qualities.

FIG. 143. Rabbit tobacco.

FIG. 144. Indian blanket (blanket flower), *Gaillardia aestivalis.*

FIG. 145. Spiny thistle, *Cirsium horridulum.*

Indian blanket (blanket flower), *Gaillardia aestivalis,* is another rhizomatous perennial of dry upland pine woodlands and prairie grasslands. It is a high C-value (10-ranked) sunflower species that attracts butterflies, wasps, and bees for its nectar and pollen. It also attracts nectar-seeking hummingbirds, and other birds eat the seed.[177] Its range encompasses the southern United States from Kansas to Texas, eastward to Florida, and northward to the Carolinas.[178]

Spiny (bull) thistle, *Cirsium horridulum,* is a biennial to perennial forb and member of the sunflower family that grows to six or more feet in height.[179] Its stems are edible for humans, and it is an excellent plant for nectar- and pollen-seeking bees and other insects. Yet I still do a double take when I see a delicate butterfly perched on the wicked thistles, gathering nectar and pollen from the flowers. Hummingbirds, too, are able to gather the nectar, and the plants are host to little metalmark and painted lady butterflies.[180] Birds eat the plant's seed. Spiny thistle prefers moist, well-drained soil. Its range encompasses Central America and Mexico, the southern Midwest, and mostly coastal plain states farther east and up the east coast.[181]

Solidago, the goldenrod genus. The goldenrod genus is one of the most well-known genera of the sunflower family because it contains so many large and showy wildflowers. Most of our goldenrods bloom in the fall. They must be one of the champions of the fall nectar- and pollen-providing plants, as their large blooms are visited by bees, butterflies, wasps, flies, and humming-birds.[182] Several species of moths and checkerspot butterflies use goldenrods as host plants.[183] Wafer Creek Ranch is fortunate to be home to at least ten species, two of which presently remain unclassified. The goldenrods have been unjustly accused of causing allergies, but ragweed, with its easily wind-borne pollen, is the real perp.

Giant goldenrod, *Solidago gigantea,* is a low C-value perennial forb and one of the more com-mon species in the genus. It's an important plant for insects (such as bees and butterflies) and also for birds, deer, and rabbits. Giant goldenrod is host to several species of beetles and moths, and birds use the flowers as natural bird feeders.[184] Goldenrods can be difficult to identify by the flowers, but a good field mark of this species is the glaucous (whitish-waxy) stem. Giant gold-enrod has a very large range covering most of North America, including northeastern Mexico. Also growing on Wafer Creek Ranch is *Solidago altissima,* variously called common goldenrod, tall goldenrod, or Canada goldenrod. Both giant and tall goldenrods are the largest plants of the genus on Wafer Creek Ranch, and both can be rather weedy.

FIG. 146. Giant goldenrod, *Solidago gigantea* Notice the light grayish-white (glaucous) stems, helpful in identification of this species.

Sweet goldenrod (anise-scented goldenrod), *Solidago odora,* is a high C-value perennial wildflower. In fact, it's likely that the rest of the goldenrods to follow (six of them, including this species) are all high C-value. So we have now arrived in the goldenrod high-rent district. Wafer Creek Ranch is special in no small way due to its rather unique group of goldenrod species. Though sweet goldenrod is quite common in North Louisiana, it exists in very large numbers on Wafer Creek Ranch and is its most common goldenrod species. The species name, *odora,* comes from the leaves of the plant being highly aromatic, and when crushed, they give off the sweet odor of licorice—an excellent field mark. Also, the leaves are quite narrow, another distinction of the species. As with the rest of the goldenrods, sweet goldenrod is a major attractor of birds seeking seeds and insects seeking nectar and pollen. Its native range is coastal Mexico, the southern Midwestern states, and the southeastern states.[185]

FIG. 147. *Right:* Sweet goldenrod, *Solidago odora.*

FIG. 148. *Below:* Louisiana goldenrod, *Solidago ludoviciana.* The lower part of the plant has fat leaves. The floral buds (flowers) are arranged in rows along a non-branching stem, forming the pattern of inflorescence called a raceme.

Louisiana goldenrod, *Solidago ludoviciana,* is a fairly large perennial goldenrod having long inflorescences (racemes) and prominent broad leaves usually restricted to the lower third of the plant—a good field mark. Its native range is restricted to Louisiana, Texas, and Arkansas.[186] The plants on Wafer Creek Ranch represent a new species for Lincoln Parish; however, the species is present in neighboring parishes. Louisiana goldenrod has abundant blooms providing nectar and pollen for insects; birds eat those insects as well as the plants' seeds. Louisiana goldenrod is fortunately quite common on Wafer Creek Ranch and it is easily spread by seeding in, which consists of gathering seed where it's common and spot planting on scratched ground, or by spreading it over recently burned bare-ground sites.

FIG. 149. Western rough goldenrod, *Solidago radula.*

FIG. 150. Downey ragged goldenrod, *Solidago petiolaris.*

Western rough goldenrod, *Solidago radula,* is a perennial forb of the southern Midwestern states, with only a few widely scattered and isolated sites farther east.[187] As with the other goldenrods, it's a provider of nectar and pollen for insects and the seeds are eaten by birds. The leaves are hairy and scratchy, giving the "rough" description to this goldenrod.

Downey ragged goldenrod, *Solidago petiolaris,* is a perennial forb having a range encompassing part of Mexico, the southern Midwest, and the coastal southern states.[188] Downey ragged is host plant to a variety of insects, including moths, and it provides nectar and pollen to bees, butterflies, moths, beetles, and flies. The seed is eaten by small birds such as buntings and sparrows, and deer and rabbits browse the young foliage.[189] Like several of the goldenrods on Wafer Creek Ranch, they are only locally common, but I gather the seeds in the fall and distribute them in the many sites where the plant presently doesn't exist. Most of the upland soils on Wafer Creek Ranch are acid, which is preferred by downy ragged.

Wrinkleleaf goldenrod, *Solidago rugosa,* is, in my opinion, appropriately named. The leaves really do have a wrinkled appearance, because of their pronounced veining pattern (figure 151). *Rugosa,* which literally means "wrinkled," comes from "rugal," a term used in human anatomy—we might speak, for example, of the rugal folds of the inner lining of the stomach. Wrinkleleaf goldenrod is a perennial forb with a range extending from the southern Mid-

FIG. 151. Wrinkleleaf goldenrod, *Solidago rugosa.* Notice the prominent wrinkling of the leaves due to the veining pattern.

FIG. 152. Shiny (flat-top) goldenrod, *Solidago nitida.* Notice the flat-topped appearance of the flowers and the thin, shiny leaves.

west and throughout the eastern United States and into eastern Canada.[190] Important to nectar- and pollen-seeking insects, they attract birds that feed on the insects, and indigo buntings, sparrows, and other seed eaters feed on its seeds. Mammals such as deer and rabbits also browse the leaves. Wrinkleleaf is a host plant to a variety of insects, including several moth species.[191]

Shiny (flat-top) goldenrod, *Solidago nitida,* is the eighth and last species classified so far on the Wafer Creek Ranch (two species remain unclassified). A perennial, it thrives in well-drained soils of the uplands and has a native range that encompasses Arkansas, Mississippi, Oklahoma, Texas, and Louisiana. The species has been found primarily in the western part of Louisiana, including three of the parishes surrounding Lincoln, but the specimen in figure 152 represents the first Lincoln Parish identification, thanks to Louisiana State University botanists Lowell Urbatsch and Chris Reid. So far, shiny goldenrod is the only Wafer Creek Ranch *Solidago,* other than sweet goldenrod, that has long, thin leaves. But the leaves of sweet goldenrod are highly fragrant, and those of shiny goldenrod are shiny. Shiny goldenrod's faunal associations are insect pollinators, including bees. Deer and rabbits browse the leaves and stems, and seed-eating birds such as juncos and sparrows eat the plant's seeds. The source of much of this information is my Acadian-French friend and emeritus US Geological Survey botanist Larry Allain, who explains that the name goldenrod was called by the Acadian people verge d'or—literally, rod (or branch) of gold.[192]

Little Plant Diversity "Hot Spots"

The collection of grasses and wildflowers shown on the preceding pages represents only a few of the individuals that thrive in the Wafer Creek Ranch grassland. But, in part because of my seeding-in technique, those grass and wildflower species are now beginning to form a few small but enlarging patches of plant diversity, or "hot spots." It's nice to see this, because it obviously means the restoration is working. Photos of these little patches give us the chance to see these species in their environment rather than individu-

FIG. 153. Here's a gang of grassland species: little bluestem, slender Indiangrass, elegant blazing star, four goldenrod species (Louisiana, wrinkleleaf, sweet, and giant), and others. Scenes with this level of species diversity are slowly beginning to become more numerous on Wafer Creek Ranch. Imagine the insect species that follow the food sources provided by these grassland plants. This is part of what makes restoration of an ecosystem so rewarding.

FIG. 154. Species in this photo include white-leaf mountain mint, little bluestem, elegant blazing star, sweet goldenrod, Louisiana goldenrod, soft golden aster, and partridge pea.

ally relegated into separate photos and descriptions. When we can see them surrounded by their neighbors and thriving in their own grassland settings, they create scenes reminiscent of little wildflower gardens.

Earlier in this work, I asked why we should protect and restore an ecosystem. The best answer that I know is that ecosystem protection and restoration are truly vital tools we can use in the rescue of our vanishing biodiversity—of plants, birds, mammals, reptiles, amphibians, insects, arachnids, worms, mollusks, fungi, and so many others. This is especially true when the ecosystem includes a grassland groundcover, for it is well known that such groundcovers are especially rich in floral and faunal species—especially grasslands of the South!

How large must a tract of land be to be big enough to restore? Of course, the bigger the better, but in my opinion, nothing is too small. The area on Wafer Creek Ranch permanently protected by a Nature Conservancy conservation easement is four hundred acres of a mixture of bottomland hardwood forest, forested draws, and lower slopes and the upland ridges and plateaus and their upper slopes, which are the zones of the historic shortleaf pine-oak-hickory woodland and grassland.

The historic shortleaf pine-oak-hickory woodland zones of the uplands are *for the most part* now in about 160 to 165 acres of active woodland and groundcover restoration. This certainly is a large area for me to try to tackle, but in truth, it's tiny in comparison with the massive size of the historic upland grasslands that could be restored in the Upper West Gulf Coastal Plain or the southeastern United States![1]

Urban areas, backyards, school grounds, parks, and the like are, to me, fair game for establishing native plant species to attract insects, birds, small mammals, reptiles, and others. Whenever I see a highway, pipeline, or electric power line right-of-way, I see potential for the establishment of a native grassland groundcover. The same could be said for almost any patch of unutilized ground.

Lady Bird Johnson was a visionary in rescuing biodiversity nearly six decades ago, as she captivated scientists and the public with her plea to eliminate the usual nonnative turf grasses along highway rights-of-way and replace them with native wildflower species. It was because of Lady Bird that the Highway Beautification Act of 1965 came to be. Sadly, other than a few scattered flowers (many of which are nonnatives), I see little evidence of her magnificent dream these days in my state. The potential for grassland restoration and its rescue of biodiversity along interstate highways is massive.

A good friend of mine, Peggy Grau, with whom I attended grammar school, junior high, and high school, plants native milkweed in her yard and collects the leaves when she finds monarch butterfly eggs on the leaf surfaces. She brings the leaves into her house and arranges them in butterfly cages to protect the caterpillars from possible predators in her yard, as she believes she is detecting some caterpillar losses; then she feeds them more milkweed leaves as they grow. When the caterpillars mature into adult butterflies, she releases them to go their genetically predetermined way. In my mind Peggy is a hero, because she is rescuing an imperiled species one butterfly at a time. She is doing a good thing. She's doing her part.

III

The Protection and Restoration of Wafer Creek Ranch

How It All Began

Back in a time not long after the turn of the twenty-first century, I (on horseback in those days) came to realize that Wafer Creek Ranch was special, and not simply because I had a sentimental attachment to it. In the first place, I could see that it had an old-growth mixed forest of shortleaf pines and hardwoods—its old hickories really stood out. I also realized that this was uncommon in our present-day landscape. After all, it was obvious that much of the countryside was being converted to short-rotation loblolly pine plantations. That bothered me.

I had always expressed my objections to my father with regard to any consideration of selling timber on the family land, even before he inherited it from my grandmother. After her death in 1983, the old family land was divided four ways, with my father gaining a full quarter of the property. (It was one hundred years earlier, in the late 1880s, when my great-great grandfather J. W. Horton began buying the property to start a cotton farm, and my grandmother was born on it in 1899.) Even when the land belonged to my father, whenever he brought up the subject of selling timber, I continued to object. Thank goodness he always graciously yielded to my wishes. And not long after that time, he decided to donate the land to me. As well, my father and mother and Karen and I, together, added another 270 acres of adjoining land that had once been under ownership of my grandmother's aunt Hattie. And once again, my father, mother, and Karen deeded that land over to me. To this day I am profoundly grateful for their generosity and expression of faith in my stewardship.

But early on, my stewardship abilities crapped out thoroughly. I made a fat F on the day I signed a lease with an oil company, under the mistaken belief that the lease had what was expressed to me as "essentially" a no-drill clause. The hard lesson I learned was this: never sign anything based on what an oil and gas company representative, or a landman working on its behalf, conveys without first consulting an expert landman or attorney who works on *your* behalf.

If there's anything good to say about this boondoggle, for which I take full responsibility, it is that the well that was drilled on Wafer Creek Ranch destroyed only about one acre of forest, as it occurred back in the days before the fracking boom began in Lincoln Parish. A well to accommodate fracking would have resulted in at least five times the destruction. Nevertheless, the site is a blemish and a sour reminder of my rank naïveté.

In spite of my stumble in the early days, much of Wafer Creek Ranch had a mixture of old-growth shortleaf pines and lots of upland hardwoods—old-growth upland oaks and hickories. It was beautiful and special, certainly in comparison to what was present in the surrounding countryside. And I was the solitary owner of the property. I began to think about the significance of the power I had over the fate of that forest, and I came to realize that if any one person had the opportunity to save it, it would be me. That became a moral issue and I realized that it was up to me, and me alone, to do whatever I could to try to save that beautiful old-growth forest.

It doesn't take much forethought to realize that if an old-growth forest, or any other natural landscape, is not permanently protected, it will one way or another be destroyed at some point in the future. Murphy's Law. If Wafer Creek Ranch ever fell into the hands of someone who saw it as a commodity rather than what it truly was—a historic relic of a part of the original ecosystem—it would be over, and there is no shortage of people who see old-growth forests as nothing more than a dollars-and-cents commodity. The mechanism of the forest's downfall would likely be logging, oil and gas incursions, and with the growing towns of Ruston and Grambling nearby, development.

Permanent protection of the eastern portion of Wafer Creek Ranch wasn't easy. Almost half of the land was tied up in underground mineral ownership by multiple family members who refused to sign a surface waiver that would have disallowed oil and gas incursions for the benefit of protecting the natural heritage of the land. But with help from professionals who were dedicated to protecting it (expert oil and gas landman Logan Hunt and oil and gas legal expert Matt May), stronger and stronger protection of the old-growth forest began to win the day. It took years to accomplish, but I knew I could never walk away without success. And it finally, in stages, came together.

Because of negotiations with oil companies pertaining to three separate tracts of Wafer Creek Ranch over several years, the conservation easement protection is broken into three separate stand-alone easements, so it's a little messy. One might say we did it the cowboy way: it ain't pretty, but we got 'er done.

In 2005, long before the creation of the conservation easements, Nature Conservancy of Louisiana biologist Dan Weber and botanist and restoration ecologist Latimore Smith came to see whatever natural conditions existed on Wafer Creek Ranch. Generally, The Nature Conservancy does not make a commitment to protection unless a particular property has significant biological value. I knew this, and it worried me. Of course, *I* knew Wafer Creek Ranch was special, because it had so much old-growth forest on its hills, draws, and bottomlands. But would *they* be impressed?

As it turned out, Latimore saw what I was seeing right off the bat, but with a much more sophisticated eye than I had. However, it wasn't so much the bottomland that caught his attention. What impressed Latimore was its upland forest. It was loaded (at least relatively speaking) with old-growth shortleaf pines and upland hardwoods—the seven species discussed earlier in this book. He knew of no other upland forest in Louisiana that contained so much of the complete old-growth overstory of the shortleaf pine-oak-hickory woodland.

What Latimore found on the hilltops of Wafer Creek Ranch that day back in 2005 he would later describe as a "genuine rarity." And when he wrote his Wafer Creek Ranch restoration management plan for The Nature Conservancy in March 2006, he said, "What is arguably the most significant ecological feature on Wafer Creek Ranch remains: many older shortleaf pine trees (estimate many near or greater than 100 years old) scattered within the forests across the hills. It is possible that some of these trees were present in the original forest prior to clearing of the 'virgin forest'; thus, they may represent living legacies of the original forest of this land. It is highly unusual today to find sizable upland tracts in North Louisiana that support such a major component of 'old growth' shortleaf pine."[1]

For me, the lesson here is clear: if these zones of Wafer Creek Ranch, as Lat described them, were ever subjected to oil and gas exploitation, devel-

FIG. 155. Field botanist and restoration ecologist Latimore Smith.

FIG. 156. The relic old-growth shortleaf pine-oak-hickory woodland overstory on Wafer Creek Ranch.

opment, or the forestry practice of clear-cutting, or even selective cutting without regard for the ecological features of the land, Wafer Creek Ranch would never have had its protection or its restoration of its shortleaf pine-oak-hickory woodland.

Latimore described the old-growth overstory on Wafer Creek Ranch as a genuine rarity not because it harbored a significant historical site or a sacred Native American landmark or even an endangered species. It simply was a rare leftover from the dirty shame of our overexploited landscape.

Based on his findings in 2005, Latimore, being the restoration ecologist he is, wanted to begin the restoration right away. Before he left that day, he was already developing an action plan, seeing with his mind's eye the grassland groundcover, especially "little bluestem swaying in the breeze."

But that was a dream to come long in the future. I had no idea what I was getting into with 160 acres of active restoration to face. After all, that beautiful overstory was, due to long years of fire suppression, buried in a dense forest, crowded by those native species normally residing downslope but that, over time, had gradually crept uphill. Under all that shade, no woodland groundcover existed.

Latimore was now the captain. I was first mate with no experience. And I was the only other sailor on the ship.

The first move by Latimore was to contact the Louisiana Department of Wildlife and Fisheries to tip them off about his findings on Wafer Creek Ranch. Soon after, Dan Weber, Latimore, and I met on Wafer Creek Ranch with a small group of people from LDWF, which would lead to the ranch becoming a state registered natural area in 2006. One of the department members who was there that day was then-LDWF botanist Chris Reid, who would later become a close friend and, along with Latimore, one of my top go-to people for plant identification to this day. My expert sources list was growing. Things were beginning to roll.

The beginning point of a succession of restoration activities in Latimore's plan of action was a timber cut executed according to his specifications. Logging is messy and causes damage through soil disturbance and injury to surrounding trees. So it must be done in a way that preserves whatever shortleaf pines and upland hardwood species exist. But the logging was needed to remove an overabundance of loblolly pine as well as whatever "off-site" fire-sensitive species the loggers would take with them. Examples of such species include loblolly pine (*Pinus taeda*), sweet gum (*Liquidambar styraciflua*), red maple (*Acer rubrum*), southern sugar maple (*Acer floridanum*), winged elm (*Ulmus alata*), black gum (*Nyssa sylvatica*), American holly (*Ilex opaca*), devil's walking stick (*Aralia spinosa*), American hornbeam (*Carpinus caroliniana*), hop-hornbeam (*Ostrya virginiana*), American beech (*Fagus grandifolia*), eastern red-cedar (*Juniperus virginiana*), water oak (*Quercus nigra*),

FIG. 157. The native mixed hardwood-loblolly pine forest community of the lower slopes and draws. These native downslope forests have dense canopies with abundant shade and a sparse groundcover. Fires burn cooler here because there's no grass groundcover.

FIG. 158. *Right:* Water oak is a typical fire-sensitive species of bottomland forests where the small stream forest community exists. But after many years of fire suppression, these fire-sensitive oaks grow up to become big trees in the uplands.

FIG. 159. *Below:* Winged sumac is one of several "off-site" shrub species that, as a result of fire suppression, will overtake the woodland grassland, shading out grasses and forbs.

black cherry (*Prunus serotina*), and shrubs such as winged sumac (*Rhus co-pallinum*), American beautyberry/French mulberry (*Callicarpa americana*), saltbush (*Baccharis halimifolia*), and the invasive native herb cypress weed (*Eupatorium capillifolium*).

It's likely that about 40 percent to 50 percent of the upland area of Wafer Creek Ranch is not damaged by agriculture of the past. That is, it was never plowed, although in the days long past, part of it was undoubtedly logged, primarily by selective thinning. These upland zones thus retain all the members of the historic woodland overstory, which includes the old-growth shortleaf pines and the seven relatively fire-tolerant upland hardwood species. These are the zones of Wafer Creek Ranch with a relic old-growth shortleaf pine-oak-hickory overstory that initially excited Latimore back in 2005.

Unfortunately, there was no grassland groundcover. Due to so many years of fire suppression, it had long ago been shaded out by the native off-sites.

In the upland zones that had been plowed, the historic woodland overstory was extirpated entirely. Today, some of that has grown back, but most of it was eventually replaced and, due to fire suppression, dominated by the downslope fire-sensitive species. (Unfortunately, even older-growth mixed forests of sixty years or older have become increasingly uncommon over the countryside, due to the unfortunate practice of clear-cutting. The Upper West Gulf Coastal Plain ecoregion today bears essentially no resemblance to the landscape that existed 250 years ago).

FIG. 160. Much of the countryside of the Upper West Gulf Coastal Plain looks like this today—off-site species dominant, in large part because of the current practices of the forestry industry and of landowners who may not realize the ecological value of their property.

Actions on Wafer Creek Ranch to Reestablish the Native Ecosystem

Basically, the actions required to restore a native woodland grassland within an overgrown dense forest of the Upper West Gulf Coastal Plain occur in three stages. First, the off-site species are removed by logging and targeted herbicide. This is followed by fire, and eventually by seeding in with native herbaceous grassland species.

LOGGING AND HERBICIDE

There have been two major logging events on Wafer Creek Ranch, in 2007 and 2009. A much smaller event took place around 2012 in a zone where the original cut was inadequate and eventually needed further loblolly removal to open up the woodland. The goal of the logging was to let in enough sunlight for the establishment of the grassland groundcover and to give more space for the growth of the shortleaf pines and upland hardwood species.

With each of the logging events, the loggers took away most of the mature loblolly pines and off-site hardwood trees, but the smaller, younger trees and species that did not reach a size and quality to be taken to the mill were left behind for me to deal with by means of herbicide application. Some of the larger loblolly specimens were left behind for needle fall, in order to carry fire, but over time I've also had to herbicide most of these as the fire-carrying grasses began to take their role and the need for pine needles became less important.

I call my own method of herbicide application for trees "hack and paint." I chop a ring completely around the trunk and, using a paintbrush, paint in the herbicide at full industrial strength. Such a method of tree herbicide application *seems* to have an extremely small impact on the environment. I can obtain my chemicals from herbicide supply houses, and occasionally from feed and garden stores, where I always buy it in 2.5-gallon jugs.[1] The herbicide I presently use is triclopyr, which comes under several brand names, including Garlon 4. Garlon 4 seems not to work well in killing older-growth loblolly pines, but my experience with its use for that purpose is lacking. If I want to kill a loblolly pine today, I would use 41 percent glyphosate with my hack-and-paint method.

I use Garlon 4 for targeted foliage application during the warm months. Dormant-season stem application in winter requires mixing the chemical with an oil compound, at a mixture with a higher herbicide concentration than that of my foliar treatment. This method requires spraying the stems of the off-site shrubs and small trees, which works quite well, and during the dormant season the problem of the fumes killing young forb species is minimized. Although herbicide application in spring is somewhat effective, it is less so than application during summer, fall, and winter. Herbicide people and foresters say that spring is the time of upward sap flow, which can interfere with the herbicide reaching the roots. But possibly more important is waiting for maximum stem development and leaf size, which in North Louisiana only occurs in the second half of spring. The greater the leaf surface, the more herbicide is absorbed by the plant.

Both shrub stem application and foliage application leave a certain amount of herbicide on the ground, but the half-life of triclopyr in the soil is about one to three months, so it doesn't last as long as some of the other chemicals on the market. Sadly, targeted spraying always creates a significant amount of collateral damage to the all-important grasses and forbs, and the triclopyr fumes left in the air, though not harmful to grasses, can be lethal to forbs in the immediate area during the warm months, especially to goldenrods and some other composites.

In all honesty, I must say that the use of toxic chemicals in a restoration of grasses and forbs seems barbaric and counterintuitive. I wish it were not necessary, but it is simply a must. Worse was the realization that I couldn't just do it once and have it be over. Oh, how I wish it were so. Every year—spring, summer, fall, and winter—it seems I have to go out and face the same fearsome task, and at this point I realize that it might never end. But I can also say there's a bright side: during the summer and fall, I am able to identify more and more forb and grass species and to give myself the opportunity to actually see up close the progress of the restoration, largely due to my herbicide work.

As I have said, the main obstacle I face is the many native invasive species, such as American beautyberry (if invasive to a site), winged sumac, young native off-site tree species, cypress weed (dog fennel), saltbush, devil's walking stick, and yaupon (if invasive to a site), along with a few others, if they are exhibiting invasive growth.

Wafer Creek Ranch also has its share of nonnative species—many, in fact. However, the majority are not invasive to a degree that they cause real damage to the ecosystem. The most fearsome organism on Wafer Creek Ranch, in my opinion, is *Lygodium japonicum,* commonly called Japanese climbing fern. It's a monster, and if you don't believe it, look online and see what it can do. The pictures there will show monstrous examples of what is left of the ground and trees completely covered by the vine, which leaves behind grotesque scenes. It is notoriously difficult to kill because of its rapid growth, rhizomatous spread, and the multitude of spores produced from the sporangia of the leaves. It seems to "pop up," as if spontaneous generation were actually real. Other easier-to-manage introduced invasive species that I have to kill are Brazilian blue vervain, sericea lespedeza (*Lespedeza cuneata*), Chinese privet, the occasional Chinese tallow tree, and a few others.

In Latimore's restoration plan, he wrote that the restoration of Wafer Creek Ranch would be largely a "learn as we go" process. This has certainly been the case.

It is shocking to me just how much herbicide work, season after season, year after year, is required to keep up with the native and nonnative invasive

FIG. 161. Japanese climbing fern, *Ligodium japonicum.*

tree, shrub, and herbaceous species infestations that just keep coming up in sites that, two years prior, were apparently "clean" because of my former herbicide application. It has become very difficult to for me to simply keep up with a 160-acre restoration. The message is this: restoration of damaged woodlands in the Upper West Gulf Coastal Plain may need a very large amount of herbicide work over a long period before controlled burning can rein in the invaders. And before that can happen, a large and healthy groundcover of little bluestem grass will likely be required.

FIG. 162. *Left:* A recently logged site in need of foliage and stem herbicide application followed up with more herbicide over time.

FIG. 163. *Below:* A fairly recently logged site without herbicide. No grassland groundcover can survive in this mess. Winged sumac in foreground; small trees in background are sweet gums. Both are native invasive off-site species.

CONTROLLED BURNING

According to Latimore Smith, it's likely that natural lightning strikes or fires induced by Native people occurred at an average interval of only about every five to ten years in the historic shortleaf pine-oak-hickory woodland. But a young ongoing restoration, as is the case with Wafer Creek Ranch, requires more.

Presently, the standard for WCR is a dormant-season to occasional growing-season burn at a two-year fire rotation, that is, burning every other year. Annual burning could be sustained on Wafer Creek Ranch because of the lush growth of its groundcover and would even likely be better for inducing the growth of grasses. However, entomological studies, particularly one conducted by Ron Panzer, have shown that annual burns have a negative impact on a subset of overwintering insects. The eggs that spend the cold months in leaf litter on the ground will burn up in a fire, and some of those insect populations don't have time to fully recover over the course of a year. However, a two-year fire rotation is apparently adequate for full insect recovery.[2] Even so, as Latimore said, we learn as we go, so we must always be nimble and ready to change strategies as needed, especially those pertaining to fire and herbicide.

FIG. 164. Controlled understory fire on Wafer Creek Ranch.

When an area that for many years has been densely shaded by off-site trees and shrubs is finally "cleaned" through logging, herbicide application, and controlled burns, it likely will be left with a paucity of native grasses and forbs. This is the time to take an inventory of native grasses and wildflower species that might be present in order to determine whether seeding the site with little bluestem and other grasses, as well as herbaceous wildflower species, is needed. If so, what plants are lacking and what plants most need to be seeded in?

Remember, little bluestem is a "matrix" grass of the woodland grassland ecosystem, as well as of the majority of all grasslands of the Midwest and southern states. In this context, it is the most important species because of its historical dominance of the ecosystem and its vital role as a carrier of fire. But any seeds of noninvasive native grasses and wildflowers can be added to the mix.

Where the new seeds come from is an important subject. It may be that seeds ordered from seed suppliers would not be a wise choice, as often the seed from these sources have been genetically modified in some manner in order to bring out certain traits, such as increased size and/or germination rate, which might foster unintended aggressiveness within an ecosystem. Plus, even if it's pure wild seed, it is unlikely that the seed would be of the same ecotype as that of the location to be restored. Many restoration ecologists are convinced that an introduced ecotype foreign to a particular ecotypic region loses its vitality over time and can even cause the loss of vitality within the progeny of crossbreeding with the native ecotype.

Whether or not the introduction of a foreign ecotype of a species is a biologically acceptable practice is perhaps debatable. However, Latimore is a purist regarding this subject, and I'm most comfortable with his approach. We have decided that ecotype purity is our choice throughout the process of seeding in, and only seed from Wafer Creek Ranch itself or from Lincoln and surrounding parishes has been used. The seeds are gathered by hand from Wafer Creek Ranch, local roadsides, and power line rights-of-way. Such small grassland sites often have a nice diversity of forbs and grasses, including sometimes an abundance of little bluestem, splitbeard bluestem, and Elliott's bluestem as well as interesting native forbs such as blazing stars and high C-value goldenrods. Although this method is slow, due to the limited quantity of seed of both the grasses and forbs that I am able to gather each year, over time it has made a difference.

But more little bluestem is badly needed, and in the fall of 2019, the stars aligned just right for Wafer Creek Ranch. Through an amazing amount of effort, knowledge of the system, and contacts, Latimore scored a big win. He was able to get help and coordination from Chris Doffitt, botanist with LDWF; the University of Louisiana–Lafayette and its employee Jacob Matthews; US Geological Survey field botanist Larry Allain; and Dave Moore, botanist for the Catahoula District Kisatchie National Forest in Louisiana.

It turns out that Kisatchie has a system of large fields containing abundant little bluestem, and it's the same ecotype that is present on Wafer Creek Ranch and surrounding areas. Coordinating the harvest was complex, to say the least, but everything was lined up for liftoff in the fall of 2018—everything, that is, except the weather. The window for harvesting little bluestem seed is small. Ultimately, in 2018 we lost our window due to weather noncompliance—too much rain.

But it all worked out in the fall of 2019. The tractor with mounted seed harvester (compliments of University of Louisiana–Lafayette) was driven and operated by Jacob Matthews. Jacob harvested the seed and periodically dropped his loads off on tarps for Latimore, Larry, and me to spread out for sun drying. At task's end, I drove my trailer with the rolled tarps of seed ("burritos," as Latimore calls them) back to Wafer Creek Ranch for further drying, and we ultimately wound up with thirty-five burlap sacks of seed—a good haul for three old men working in the effort to rescue biodiversity.

If a site is not overly degraded, or at least lies close to a seed source, a "clean" site (after logging, fire, and herbicide) that is apparently species-sparse fortunately will recover with numbers of native grass and forb species without the need for seeding in. And sometimes those "self-regenerating" forbs and grasses will have a high C-value.

How does this happen on a clean site that has only sparse groundcover after all those years of fire suppression? These grass and wildflower species (sometimes with high C-value) are certainly not to be found on a clean site. So, what's up, Doc? Where did they come from?

FIG. 165. *Left to right:* Latimore Smith, Jacob Matthews, Larry Allain, Dave Moore, and my trailer behind them.

BIRDS, MAMMALS, INSECTS, AND WIND

Combined, birds, mammals, insects, and wind lead to a significant level of seeding in. Birds and mammals carry, drop, and defecate seeds when they move from one site to another. Squirrels and other rodents actually stash or dig small holes and plant the seed or nuts. Interestingly, some species of ants disperse seeds.[3] And many seeds, due to their structure, are easily carried in the wind.

SEED BANK

Also significantly, the seed bank is a phenomenon by which seeds of certain species of grasses and forbs can remain viable in the soil for years and then eventually germinate and sprout when conditions such as availability of sunlight, moisture, and fire are present. However, research has shown that many high C-value perennial species do not form long-lived seed banks.[4]

BUD BANK

On Wafer Creek Ranch the concept of the bud bank (increasingly discussed among restoration ecologists) may possibly have a noticeable application, particularly in a zone of upland old-growth forest on the west side of Wafer Creek. Although an old-growth shortleaf pine-oak-hickory overstory is intact in this location, the original woodland groundcover was lost due to many years of fire suppression, which changed the woodland into a dense, shady forest.

The bud bank is a fascinating subject in that it has been found by researchers to make a large contribution to the regeneration of degraded plant communities, often significantly more so than the contribution by the seed bank. Seed sprouts arising from the seed bank generally have a high death rate due to conditions such as availability of moisture, storms, too much direct sunlight in dry conditions, soil erosion, and predation by animals such as insects, birds, and mammals.

Meristems are clusters of noncommitted, dividing plant cells with the ability to become a variety of plant organs or even a new plant. Here, one can draw a partial analogy with the stem cells of animals, such as those located in the bone marrow and elsewhere.

Meristems are located on certain sites of the plant above ground, but many are located, or "banked," underground on plant structures such as corms, bulbs, tubers, rhizomes, stem collars, and others.[5]

In the Wafer Creek Ranch old-growth uplands of the west side of Wafer Creek, which until recently was a shady forest but now is an open short-leaf pine-oak-hickory woodland, there has been a resurgence of fairly significant numbers of high C-value forbs such as Texas ironweed, azure blue sage, white-flowered milkweed, butterfly milkweed, coral bean (technically a shrub), and at least seven of the ten known species of goldenrod on Wafer Creek Ranch. Three of those high C-value goldenrod species are located only on the west side of the creek.

For years I have wondered how all these species got there. No one planted them. It seems unlikely that birds or mammals dropped goldenrod seeds there, although I can't rule that out. However, most of the high C-value plants I've just listed, including the goldenrods, are plants with rhizomes that are underground, laterally extending, modified roots. They, in part, are members of the bud bank. Rhizomes have sites along their length where meristems are located, and these sites have the potential to produce a new plant. So the bud bank is a possible origin of these interesting species. According to Latimore, it's also possible that the seed bank has a role, or small, suppressed perennials may have been sitting in a dark forest for many years at the soil surface, producing enough leaf surface to capture the sunlight needed to sustain themselves. Maybe they were simply hiding in plain sight all along, waiting for the right conditions to make themselves known.

I suppose I'll never know for sure how that collection of plants and so many others arose in those upland old-growth woodland sites, but what I'd really like to know is just how long the ancestors of those plants have been residing in those hills. The questions keep coming up.

Results So Far on Wafer Creek Ranch

In many ways, the restoration has come far. After all, the shortleaf pine-oak-hickory woodland and grassland on Wafer Creek Ranch has been recognized as perhaps the best example of this plant community type in Louisiana.[1]

There is prima facie evidence of a significant increase in diversity and numbers of grass and wildflower species and, at least anecdotally, of insect pollinators, especially when we consider that, before the restoration, what existed was a dense and dark forest with a sparse groundcover.

A number of woodland species on the US Fish and Wildlife Service's list of Birds of Management Concern can be found on Wafer Creek Ranch. These include American kestrel, American woodcock, brown-headed nuthatch, chuck-will's-widow, field sparrow, prairie warbler, red-headed woodpecker, Henslow's sparrow, and eastern wild turkey. (Unfortunately, loggerhead shrike and northern bobwhite have not been seen in well over a decade.)[2]

The method I have used to restore the grassland on Wafer Creek Ranch may not be the only method, or even the best. For instance, careful short-rotation cattle grazing might be an effective adjunct to herbicide—cows eat Japanese climbing fern! After all, during precolonial times, large herbivores such as bison and possibly elk grazed the woodland grassland of North Louisiana. These large animals must have had a powerful and positive impact on the system as top herbivores.[3]

Today, it is rewarding to see the landscape of the historic woodland grassland taking shape and providing scenic vistas. Beautiful woodland grasslands now exist where there were none when the restoration began. The groundcover is developing, with a growing diversity of scenic wildflowers and grasses.

Hopefully, the addition and spread of little bluestem will someday outcompete some of my problem species, and hotter fires due to the dominance of little bluestem will no doubt be of benefit. But we're not there yet. It takes time, and the work must continue.

The payoff of restoration has been, and continues to be, high on Wafer Creek Ranch, and these techniques can be applied to other restorations. If humans are to save the remaining biodiversity of planet Earth, and ourselves in the process, protection and restoration of ecosystems will surely be important tools in that endeavor. And, in this way, we will be helping to ensure a healthy future for our grandchildren and the generations to come.

What follows are more photos of how the restoration looks today after nearly a decade and a half of herbicide, seeding in of native wildflowers and grasses, and controlled burns. Plus, I have thrown in a few of our fellow creatures who share Wafer Creek Ranch with Karen, Opal, Clara Eileen, and me.

So, vente conmigo! Come with me. Let's go on a little field trip.

Old-growth shortleaf pine. Some of these specimens are one hundred years old or older.

Left: Late spring: black-eyed Susans in an old-growth woodland site.

Below right: US Forest Service scientists inspect one of the large shortleaf pines on Wafer Creek Ranch. Old shortleafs like this one have become exceptionally rare finds in the forests of our countryside today.

Above: Woodland with red buckeye, an important spring-blooming midstory shrub and hummingbird plant. Opal on bear watch.

Bottom right: Scoliid wasp gathering nectar on prairie blazing star. Wasps are important pollinators in grasslands. Wasp identification thanks to Chris Carlton, entomologist, Louisiana State University.

Where once was a dark and scrambled forest is now a woodland grassland. The photo (*right*) shows late spring wild bergamot and little bluestem.

Below left: Emerald flower scarab beetles following behind a flower longhorn beetle on a white-flowered milkweed blossom. Grasslands are heaven for nectar- and pollen-gathering beetles. Beetle identifications thanks to entomologist Natalie Clay, Louisiana Tech University.

Above right: American lady butterfly, not a milkweed insect, gathering nectar from a white-flowered milkweed blossom. The blossoms of milkweed are fair game for a large variety of pollinating insects that are not dependent on milkweed as host plants.

Left: Woodland with giant goldenrod in foreground. Notice the light grayish-white (glaucous) stems. It's nice to see goldenrods blooming in an open woodland; before the restoration, this was a dark forest where goldenrods were nonexistent.

Giant swallowtail butterfly on prairie blazing star. Before the restoration began, I'm sure there must have been giant swallowtails around because their host plant, wafer ash, would have been present in the midstory. But restoration, with its wildflower nectar and pollen provisions, have brought them out in the open and is helping to sustain their population.

Granddaughter Tullie Simpkins shows the results of her seeding-in of prairie blazing star a few years earlier.

Above: Purple lovegrass on a dewy morning. On WCR, this lovegrass often occurs in patches like this, within their neighborhood of other grasses and wildflower species.

Right: The shortleaf pine-oak-hickory woodland of the west side of Wafer Creek, a zone that seems special, with several species identified that were not known to exist on the east side of the creek, even though it's a larger area. This west-side woodland has been a seed source for me in populating the east side with some important perennial wildflowers.

I think of fall as the season of yellow flowers (*right*). Maybe it's because of scenes like this one, compliments of this wrinkle-leaf goldenrod in October. Wrinkleleaf has become quite common due to the progress of the restoration.

Top left: Beeblossom, *Oenothera (Gaura) lindheimeri,* is endemic to northeastern Mexico, Texas, and Louisiana. Endemics, including those of fairly broad regions of the South, are special. They occur nowhere else on Earth!

Bottom left: The zebra swallow-tail butterfly, like this one, is dependent on pawpaw as its host plant. Wafer Creek Ranch has the common pawpaw, a small tree of the bottomlands, and dwarf pawpaw, a shrub of the shortleaf pine-oak-hickory uplands and a member of the woodland midstory.

The bowl and doily spider, a species of sheet weaver spider, weaves a bowl web and a doily (a sheet web, *below*). The spider, "hanging out" beneath the bowl, captures its insect prey as it falls through the bowl. Bowl and doily spiders thrive in grassland settings.

Left: Dwarf pawpaw, *Asimina parviflora.*

Below: Bumblebees stash pollen and nectar on their hind legs, forming an orange globoid structure called a pollen sac. The bee carries it back to the hive to distribute the pollen and nectar to the larvae.

Grass flowers, such as those of this splitbeard bluestem, have no petals. The flower parts we see are the male stamens supporting the pollen-filled anthers, and the female receptacle is called the stigma (a part of the pistil).

Here, our splitbeard bluestem grass flowers show the drooping, yellow, pollen-filled anthers (male) attached to their filaments. The stigmas (female) are the white feathery structures. Grass pollination is carried out primarily by the wind, without the need of insects, but there's an informative article by Timothy Jones telling of bees caught with their pollen sacs filled with grass pollen. Those bees have some explaining to do! Timothy Mark Jones, "Why Is the Lawn Buzzing?," *Biodiversity Data Journal,* April 2014, https://www.ncbi.nlm.nih.gov/pmc /articles/PMC4040422.

Right: The magnificent work of a spiny orb weaver spider. The little spiny spider is in the center of the web.

Below: The small, round spiny orb weaver spiders I commonly see on Wafer Creek Ranch (like the one who made the web to the right) are just under half an inch in body length. They look like little spotted crabs.

Our native tarantula, *Aphonopelma hentzi,* is called the Louisiana tarantula or Texas tarantula. This specimen, found in November of 2020 next to our house, is an unfortunate victim of Clara Eileen, our cat. Louisiana tarantulas thrive in upland grassland systems, such as that on WCR, due to the restoration.

When an orb weaver catches an insect in its web, the spider injects a toxin into the animal to paralyze it before wrapping it in a web cocoon. This large orb weaver has its grasshopper prey wrapped up. There are about 180 species of orb weavers in North America (north of Mexico), and several species of orb weavers thrive as predators in the recovering grassland on WCR.

Left: Though present in small isolated zones before the restoration began, slender Indiangrass is now becoming quite common on Wafer Creek Ranch.

Below: Pearl crescent butterflies (underwings shown) on narrowleaf mountain mint. Butterfly identification thanks to Chris Carlton, entomologist, Louisiana State University, Baton Rouge.

Above: Elegant blazing star, *Liatris elegans.* A Gulf fritillary butterfly is coming in for a landing. The more pollinator plants there are, the more pollinators and other nonpollinating insects there are. That's progress in the restoration of a grassland plant community.

Bottom right: Hemipterans, members of the insect order of true bugs, on little bluestem. These bugs are likely feeding on the little bluestem or something on it, as the bugs themselves are prey to other insects and birds. Reestablishment of the food web is a primary function of restoration.

Right: On an October morning, narrowleaf sunflowers stand out against a background of white snakeroot and splashes of sunlight. People enjoy pretty scenes of nature such as this. And who knows? Maybe such scenes will spur a few folks to take up the cause of restoring a patch of ground themselves. Don't worry about starting small!

Below: This colorful green lynx spider and her egg sac are perched on little bluestem. Madam Green Lynx is a predator, much like her mammalian lynx counterpart of the cold north.

Gulf fritillaries "puddling." Puddling gives butterflies the chance to extract moisture, salt, and minerals from damp dirt. Butterfly cannot live on nectar alone.

The Gulf fritillary is Louisiana's official state butterfly. Passion vines, its host plant, are abundant in multiple sites on WCR, and Gulf fritillaries are likewise abundant throughout the restoration.

Historically, woodlands varied in their density of trees, from those that are rather sparse in numbers of trees, such as seen in this Wafer Creek Ranch photo, and those with a higher tree density. This scene happens to be an old agriculture-damaged site lacking in old-growth upland hardwoods and short-leaf pines. But look at that grassland!

Left: A woodland setting with narrowleaf sunflower in foreground. Another striking scene of nature bound to inspire.

Above: Bidens sunflowers are usually swarming with insects, especially bees. To me, the blossoms of Bidens don't quite attain the bright glow-yellow of the narrow-leaf sunflower.

A Wafer Creek Ranch woodland in fall. Notice that there's a denser stand of old-growth trees here (*above*). This site was never plowed in the past.

Skipper butterfly on azure blue sage. Skippers (of the family Hesperiidae) likely represent some of the most common of the butterflies that thrive in the WCR restoration. I can identify only one—and the one on the azure blue sage isn't it.

Azure blue sage growing in a woodland grassland site. For thousands of years this site was a woodland grassland, later to become a cotton field, before it became a dense forest. Now, with restoration, it's a woodland grassland again.

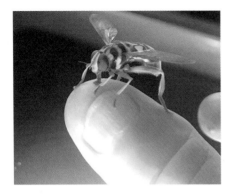

Left: It is said to be good luck to have a flower fly (hover fly) perch on your finger (excuse the blue marking dye on mine). The harmless adult flies feed on nectar and pollen and do not have stingers. They seem curious and friendly and I always enjoy their company. Flies are significant pollinators of the restoration.

Below right: White-flowered milkweed is also called red-ringed milkweed, but you have to look closely to see the red rings. This species can justly be called WCR's monarch butterfly factory.

Red-banded hairstreak butterfly on whiteleaf mountain mint. These butterflies are thumbnail-size "fast flitters," quickly moving from flower to flower, making them difficult to photograph. I've seen these hairstreaks on whiteleaf mountain mint on more than one occasion.

The eastern hognose snake is an important reptile citizen of the woodland grassland. Full of comical antics, such as spreading the skin of its head like a cobra, hissing, striking, and rolling over playing dead, it nevertheless is completely harmless and rarely (if ever) even attempts to bite. But it loves to eat toads, according to Louisiana Tech herpetologist Don Shepard.

Right: Black hickories in fall color. This is one of those spectacular scenes of nature that can only be found in an old-growth forest or woodland. This scene speaks to the importance of protection.

Below: Pipevine swallowtail butterfly on prairie blazing star.

December afternoon sunshine lights up the fan-shaped spathes of Elliott's bluestem, a high C-value warm season bunchgrass of the ecosystem.

Woodland grassland in fall. The groundcover here is mostly broomsedge, but it has recently been seeded in with little bluestem, which we hope will take charge in the years to come.

Left: Rough dropseed grass blowing in the wind. The bright, open sheaths and leaves stand out as a good field mark of this high C-value warm season bunchgrass of the restoration.

Below: Beetles are pollinators too! White-flowered milkweed blossom with a flower longhorn beetle gathering nectar and pollen. Beetle identification thanks to Natalie Clay, Louisiana Tech entomologist.

Above: Shortleaf pines today are dwindling in numbers. They need a little more respect.

Bottom right: Silver-spotted skipper on prairie blazing star. Many butterfly, moth, and bee species are long-tongued insects. You can see the tongue of this skipper as it makes a right angle to slip into the flower's center. Long-tongued insects often are the only ones who can get to the nectar and pollen of certain plant blossoms.

My grandson, Bain Simpkins (*right*), checks his field guide while on a Wafer Creek Ranch family excursion. Field trips with family, friends, students, and organizations such as garden clubs are more important today than might be fully appreciated.

Opal on her morning grassland safari. She's a supporter of higher education.

Except for the one photo of the Kisatchie National Forest longleaf pine woodland and photos otherwise credited, all the pictures in this book were taken on Wafer Creek Ranch. But I must state that although pictures are not exactly big liars, they can nevertheless be deceivers. Their deception is what they don't show us. There's really nothing like being there. And Opal couldn't agree more.

Final Thoughts

I have been a student all my life and I plan to remain one. For me, it's an honor to carry the label. But each and every scientist and observer of nature worth her or his salt is a student and knows it, for when we engage with nature, humility is our warm and gentle friend. We must never travel without it.

For many years Wafer Creek Ranch and its zones of grassland restoration have been a laboratory for study, a living museum, where I can wander and work freely, always paying attention to what and who surrounds me.

My senses are not as acute as the many species whose neighborhood I invade. For example, I can't detect the many volatile substances that insects who live in a chemical world of pheromones and other molecules can detect. I don't have the vision of predatory birds or the ability to see ultraviolet light that bees and butterflies can see. I don't possess the hearing and odor sensitivity of most mammals, and I don't hear the vibrations that snakes can hear as sound goes through their jaws and connects with their auditory sensory organs, their inner ear and brain.

Nevertheless, I can hear the calls, wing beats, and pecking sounds of birds; the snorts of deer; the sounds of coyotes, frogs, and insects; the wind in the pines; and the forlorn little cries of eastern gray squirrels.

I can smell the many different odors of plants, such as wild bergamot and whiteleaf mountain mint, eastern agave flowers, rabbit tobacco, stinky-socks *Pluchea,* the truly camphoric odor of the crushed leaves of *Heterotheca subaxillaris* (the "other camphorweed"), the licorice odor of sweet goldenrod, the odor of a dry woodland and that of a wet one. They even seem to smell differently depending on the season.

I can feel the soft fuzz of goatweed leaves and the sandpaper scratchiness of western rough goldenrod and narrowleaf sunflower leaves. The smooth velvety beaver fur–like texture of a clump of slender Indiangrass seed always impresses me. And I can feel the bark of the various species of trees as I touch them—out of curiosity and perhaps out of some wish on my part to express my greeting.

But best of all, I can see so many wonders in the world of plants and animals. The more species I see and the more I become familiar with, the more those spectacular scenes begin to come to my attention—scenes of species in their habitat, where they carry out their life duties and make their living. Every biological realm, especially a southern woodland grassland, is truly a museum of study, learning, and pleasure.

One of my primary goals in this work was to answer the question from Louisiana Tech student Dan about why we should restore a rural landscape—even a standing old-growth, mixed upland forest composed of native species, albeit altered by humans—into something close to the native woodland grassland community that originally existed so long ago.

I hope I have, at least in part, achieved that goal. But here I think we should recognize that all old-growth, native mixed-species forests, altered or not, are important resources of the landscape. After all, they serve as necessary carbon sinks vital for combating global warming, they release oxygen into the atmosphere, they clean and give protection to freshwater sources, they protect the soil from erosion, and they provide a home to many species of plants and animals. It's no wonder I sometimes succumb to the notion that a forest is a living and breathing organism in its own right. To me the bottom line is this: if such a forest is protected, even if not restored, that's a magnificent legacy.

The Lakota name for what we call nature is Unci Maka, Grandmother Earth. So I say to my friend and fellow student, Dan, who helped Dr. Maness net birds that day so long ago on WCR, that when it comes to providing the highest level of biodiversity, Unci Maka simply did a much better job than her human children could ever dream of on their own. Perhaps restoring her ecosystems, and providing them with vital protection, is our best way to say thanks to our Grandmother Earth.

As I come to the close of my story, I can think of no better ending than one last quote from E. O. Wilson, which appeared in his book *The Diversity of Life* (1992): "And let us go beyond mere salvage to begin the restoration of natural environments, in order to enlarge wild populations and stanch the hemorrhaging of biological wealth. There can be no purpose more enspiriting than to begin the age of restoration, reweaving the wondrous diversity of life that still surrounds us."

APPENDIX 1

Louisiana Biodiversity

A PARTIAL LIST OF PLACES IN LOUISIANA FOR PEOPLE TO SEE OUR STATE'S BIODIVERSITY—OPEN TO THE PUBLIC

The Nature Conservancy of Louisiana
- Mary Ann Brown Preserve (near St. Francisville)
- Grand Isle Preserve
- Cypress Island Preserve (Breaux Bridge)

Kisatchie National Forest, especially in central Louisiana
There's the Caroline Dorman Preserve. And check with any of the district offices to find the extraordinary upland longleaf pine grasslands. Kisatchie National Forest is a national treasure!

Peveto Woods Bird and Butterfly Sanctuary along the Creole Nature Trail, maintained and reserved by the Baton Rouge Audubon Society

Cameron Prairie National Wildlife Refuge (between Cameron and Lake Charles) on both sides of Calcasieu Lake

Black Bayou Lake National Wildlife Refuge (Monroe)
This is a North Louisiana treasure with lots to do and see, even a gift shop and little museum. Trails are spectacular.

There are numerous state parks and wildlife management areas, such as the Bodcau Wildlife Management Area near Shreveport, which is not far from the Red River National Wildlife Refuge and its great hiking trails.

There are so many places to go in Louisiana to spend some time with Unci Maka. This is just a tiny list, so engage in a little online research, make some calls (it's always good to call first), and get out there!

Grasses and Forbs

Shortleaf Pine-Oak-Hickory Woodland Grasses and Forbs—
Wafer Creek Ranch, July 2022

SCIENTIFIC NAME	COMMON NAME	COEFFICIENT OF CONSERVATISM
ASPLENIACEAE	FERN	
Asplenium platyneuron	ebony spleenwort	C4
DENNSTAEDTIACEAE	FERN	
Pteridium aquilinum	bracken fern	C6
LYGODIACEAE	FERN	
Lygodium japonicum	Japanese climbing fern	nonnative
AGAVACEAE	AGAVE FAMILY	
Manfreda virginica	American aloe/eastern agave	C10
Yucca (filamentosa or *louisianensis)*	beargrass yucca	
COMMELINACEAE	DAYFLOWER FAMILY	
Commelina erecta	erect dayflower	C4
Tradescantia virginiana	Virginia spiderwort	
CYPERACEAE	SEDGE FAMILY	
Carex cephalophora	oval-leaf sedge	
Carex cherokeensis	Cherokee sedge	C3
Carex flaccosperma	blue wood sedge	
Carex spp.		
Cyperus croceus	Baldwin's flatsedge	C6
Cyperus retrofractus	rough flatsedge	rare in Louisiana

SCIENTIFIC NAME	COMMON NAME	COEFFICIENT OF CONSERVATISM
CYPERACEAE (*continued*)	SEDGE FAMILY	
Cyperus strigosus	strawcolored flatsedge	
Cuperus echinatus	globe flatsedge	
Eleocharis sp.	spikesedge sp.	
JUNCACAEA	RUSH FAMILY	
Juncus marginatus	grassleaf rush	
LILIACEAE	LILLY FAMILY	
Hypoxis sp.	yellow star-grass	
ORCHIDACEAE	ORCHID FAMILY	
Genus Spiranthes	ladies' tresses orchids	
Spiranthes spp.		
Tipularia discolor	cranefly orchid	
Listera australis	southern twayblade	
POACEAE	GRASS FAMILY	
Andropogon glomeratus	bushy bluestem	C3
Andropogon gyrans	Elliott's bluestem	C7
Andropogon gerardii	big bluestem	C9
Andropogon ternarius	splitbeard bluestem	C6
Andropogon virginicus	broomsedge bluestem	C2
Aristida oligantha	prairie threeawn	C4
Aristida purperascens	arrowfeather threeawn	C8
Bothriochola sp.		
Chasmanthium sessiliflorum	longleaf woodoats	
Chasmanthium laxum	slender woodoats	
Dichanthelium commutatum	variable panicgrass	
Dichanthelium dichotomum	cypress panicgrass	C4
Dichanthelium scoparium	velvet panicgrass	C4
Elymus virginicus	Virginia wildrye	C4
Eragrostis capillaris	lacegrass	
Eragrostis spectabilis	purple lovegrass	C5
Melica mutica	twoflower melicgrass	
Muhlenbergia capillaris	Gulf Coast muhly	C8

SCIENTIFIC NAME	COMMON NAME	COEFFICIENT OF CONSERVATISM
POACEAE (*continued*)	GRASS FAMILY	
Panicum anceps	beaked panicgrass	C2
Paspalum notatum	Bahia grass	nonnative
Paspalum setaceum	thin paspalum	C5
Paspalum urvillei	Vasey grass	nonnative
Saccharum brevibarbe var. contortum	Bentawn plumegrass	
Saccharum strictus (baldwinii)	narrow plumegrass	
Schizachyrium scoparium	little bluestem	C7
Sorghastrum elliottii	slender Indiangrass	
Sphenopholis obtusata	prairie wedgegrass	C3
Sporobolus clandestinus	rough dropseed	
Stipa avenacea	feathergrass	
Tridens flavus	purpletop grass	C3
Tridens chapmanii (crotch has hairy pulvinus)	Chapman's tridens	
Tridens strictus	longspike tridens	C4
ACANTHACEAE	ACANTHUS FAMILY	
Ruellia pedunculata vs *caroliniensis*	wild petunia	C6
ANACARDIACEAE	CASHEW FAMILY (SHRUBS)	
Rhus copallinum	winged sumac	C3
Rhus glabra	smooth sumac	
Toxicodendron radicans	poison ivy	C1
AQUIFOLIACEAE	HOLLY FAMILY (SHRUBS)	
Ilex decidua	deciduous holly	C2
Ilex vomitoria	yaupon	C2
ASCLEPIADACEAE	MILKWEED FAMILY	
Asclepias tuberosa	butterfly milkweed	C7
Asclepias variagata	white-flowered milkweed	
Asclepias amplexicaulis	blunt-leaf milkweed	
Matelea gonocarpos	anglepod	C2
Matelea decipiens	climbing milkvine	

SCIENTIFIC NAME	COMMON NAME	COEFFICIENT OF CONSERVATISM
ANNONACEAE	**PAWPAW FAMILY**	
Asimina parviflora	dwarf pawpaw	
APIACEAE	**PARSLEY/CARROT FAMILY**	
Chaerophyllum tainturieri	hairyfruit chervil	C1
Eryngium yuccifolium	rattlesnake master	C9
Sanicula (canadensis or smallii)	sanicle	
Cyclospermum leptohpylum	marsh parsley	nonnative
ASTERACEAE	**SUNFLOWER FAMILY**	
Antennaria plantaginifolia	pussytoes	
Ageratina altissima	white snakeroot	
Baccharis halimifolia	saltbush	C2
Bidens aristosa	bearded beggartick	C3
Coreopsis tinctoria	plains coreopsis "calliopsis"	
Cirsium horridulum	spiny thistle	C0
Conyza canadensis	mare's tail/horseweed	C0
Conoclinium coelestinum	ageratum/mistflower	C4
Chrysopsis pilosa	soft golden aster	C6
Elephantopus tomentosus	common elephant's foot	
Elephantopus carolinianus	Carolina elephant's foot	
Erechtites hiracifolia	fire weed	C0
Erigeron philadelphicus	Philadelphia fleabane	C0
Erigeron strigosus	prairie fleabane	
Erigeron pulchellus	hairy fleabane	
Eupatorium album	white boneset	
Eupatorium capillifolium	cypress weed/dog fennel	C0
Eupatorium serotinum	late boneset	C2
Eupatorium compositifolium (? capillifolium x serotinum)		
Eupatorium perfoliatum	common boneset	C4
Eupatorium rotundifolium	roundleaf thoroughwort	C7
Euthamia leptocephala	bushy goldentop	C5
Gaillardia aestivalis	Indian blanket	C10
Gamochaeta purpurea	spoonleaf purple everlasting	C0

SCIENTIFIC NAME	COMMON NAME	COEFFICIENT OF CONSERVATISM
ASTERACEAE (*continued*)	SUNFLOWER FAMILY	
Helenium amarum	sneezeweed	C0
Helianthus angustifolius	narrowleaf sunflower	C5
Helianthus divaricatus	rough woodland sunflower	
Heterotheca subaxillaris	camphor weed	
Hieracium gronovii	hawkweed/queendevil	
Liatris pycnostachya	prairie blazing star	C9
Liatris aspera	tall blazing star	
Liatris elegans	elegant blazing star	
Lactuca canadensis	Canada wild lettuce	
Lactuca floridana	woodland lettuce	
Packera glabella	butterweed	C0
Packera tomentosa	woolly ragwort	
Pityopsis graminifolia	narrowleaf silkgrass	C9
Pluchea camphorata	camphor weed	C3
Pseudognaphalium helleri	heller's cudweed	
Pseudognaphalium obtusifolium	rabbit tobacco	C5
Pyrrhopappas carolinanus	false dandelion	C1
Rudbeckia hirta	black-eyed Susan	C5
Rudbeckia grandifolia	rough coneflower	C8
Solidago nitida	shiny goldenrod	
Solidago odora	sweet goldenrod	C10
Solidago rugosa	wrinkle-leaf goldenrod	C10
Solidago ludoviciana	Louisiana goldenrod	
Solidago altissima	tall "Canada" goldenrod	
Solidago gigantea	giant goldenrod	
Solidago radula	western rough goldenrod	
Solidago petiolaris	downy ragged goldenrod	
Solidago spp.		
Symphyotrichum dumosum	rice button aster	C2
Symphyotrichum patens	late purple aster	C8
Symphyotrichum pilosum	oldfield aster	
Verbesina helianthoides	yellow crownbeard	
Verbesina virginica	white crownbeard	
Vernonia texana	Texas ironweed	C6

SCIENTIFIC NAME	COMMON NAME	COEFFICIENT OF CONSERVATISM
BRASSICACEAE	**MUSTARD/CABBAGE FAMILY**	
Cardamine sp.	bittercress	possibly nonnative
CAMPANULACEAE	**BLUEBELL/BELLFLOWER FAMILY**	
Lobelia appendiculata	pale lobelia	C7
Lobelia cardinalis	cardinal flower	
Lobelia puberula	downy lobelia	C7
Triodanis perfoliata	clasping Venus looking glass	C3
CAPRIFOLIACEAE	**HONEYSUCKLE FAMILY**	
Lonicera japonica	Japanese honeysuckle	nonnative
Valerianella	corn salad	
CELASTRACEAE		
Euonymus americanus	hearts-a-bustin'	
CISTACEAE	**ROCKROSE FAMILY**	
Helianthemum carolinianum	Carolina rockrose	
CLUSIACEAE	**ST. JOHN'S WORT FAMILY**	
Hypericum drummondii	nits and lice	C4
Hypericum hypericoides	St. Andrew's cross	C6
Hypericum punctatum	spotted St. John's wort	
Hypericum mutilum	dwarf St. John's wort	
Hypericum prolificum	shrubby St. John's wort	
CONVOLVULACEAE	**MORNING GLORY/ SWEET POTATO FAMILY**	
Ipomoea pandurata	wild potato vine	
Ipomoea cordatotriloba	tievine	C0
Jacquemontia tamnifolia	hairy clustervine	C0
ERICACEAE	**HEATH FAMILY**	
Vaccinium arboreum	winter huckleberry	C2
Vaccinium elliottii	Elliott's blueberry	

SCIENTIFIC NAME	COMMON NAME	COEFFICIENT OF CONSERVATISM
ERICACEAE (continued)	HEATH FAMILY	
Vaccinium stamineum	deer berry/gooseberry	
Vaccinium virgatum	smallflower blueberry	
EUPHORBIACEAE	SPURGE FAMILY	
Acalypha gracilens	threeseed mercury	
Cnidoscolus texanus	Texas bullnettle	
Croton capitatus	goatweed	
Croton glandulosus	vente conmigo	C1
Euphorbia corollata	flowering spurge	C10
Tragia urticifolia	noseburn	
FABACEAE	LEGUME FAMILY	
Amphicarpeae bracteata	hog peanut	
Centrosema virginianum	climbing/spurred butterfly pea	C6
Chamaecrista fasciculata	partridge pea	C4
Clitoria mariana	butterfly pea/Atlantic pigeon wings	
Desmodium rotundifolium	prostrate ticktrefoil	
Desmodium glabellum	Dillenius's ticktrefoil	
Desmodium spp	beggar lice	
Erythrina herbacea	coral bean/Mamou	C7
Galactia volubilis	downey milkpea	
Lespedeza cuneata	sericea lespedeza	nonnative
Lespedeza hirta	bush (hairy) lespedeza	
Lespedeza virginica	slender lespedeza	C8
Lespedeza repens	creeping lespedeza	C5
Mimosa nuttallii	sensitive briar	
Rhynchosia latifolia	prairie snoutbean	
Rhynchosia tomentosa	twining snoutbean	
Senna obtusifolia	senna/sicklepod	nonnative
Strophostyles umbellata	pink fuzzybean	C6
Stylosanthes biflora	sidebeak pencilflower	C8
Tephrosia virginiana	goat's rue	
Trifolium dubium	yellow clover	nonnative

SCIENTIFIC NAME	COMMON NAME	COEFFICIENT OF CONSERVATISM
GENTIANACEAE	GENTIAN FAMILY	
Sabatia sp.	rose gentian	
HIPPOCASTANACEAE	BUCKEYE FAMILY	
Aesculus pavia	red buckeye	
IRIDACEAE	IRIS FAMILY	
Sisyrinchium sp.	blue-eyed grass	C5
LAMINACEAE	MINT FAMILY	
Monarda fistulosa	wild bergamot	C8
Monarda punctata	spotted beebalm	C4
Pycnanthemum albescens	whiteleaf mountain mint	C6
Pycnanthemum tenuifolium	narrowleaf mountain mint	C7
Salvia azurea	azure blue sage	C10
Salvia lyrata	lyerleaf sage	C2
Trichostema dichotomum	forked bluecurls	
Prunella vulgaris	prunella	C2
Scutellaria sp.	skullcap	
Teucrium canadense	Canada germander	
MALVACEAE	MALLOW FAMILY	
Sida sp.		
Modiola caroliniana	Carolina bristlemallow	C0
MELASTOMATACEAE	MELASTOME FAMILY	
Rhexia mariana	meadow beauty	C7
MYRICACEAE	WAX MYRTLE/BAYBERRY FAMILY	
Morella cerifera	wax myrtle	C3
ONAGRACEAE	EVENING PRIMROSE FAMILY	
Oenothera (Gaura) lindheimeri	Lindheimer's beeblossom	C5
Oenothera laciniata	cutleaf primrose	
Ludwigia sp	water-primrose	
Oenothera biennis	common evening primrose	

SCIENTIFIC NAME	COMMON NAME	COEFFICIENT OF CONSERVATISM
OXALIDACEAE	WOOD SORREL FAMILY	
Oxalis stricta	yellow wood sorrel	C0
Oxalis violacea	violet wood sorrel	C4
PAPAVERACEAE	POPPY FAMILY	
Corydalis sp.	butter and eggs	
PASSIFLORACEAE	PASSION FLOWER FAMILY	
Passiflora incarnata	purple passion flower	C5
Passiflora lutea	yellow passion flower	
PLANTAGINACEAE		
Plantago sp.	wild plantain	
POLYGALACEAE	MILKWORT FAMILY	
Polygala polygama	racemed milkwort	
RANNUNCULACEAE	CROWFOOT FAMILY	
Clematis virginiana	devil's darning needles	
RHAMNACEAE	BUCKTHORN FAMILY	
Frangula caroliniana	Carolina buckthorn	
ROSACEAE	ROSE FAMILY	
Rubus trivialis	southern dewberry	C3
Rubus sp.	blackberry	
RUBIACEAE	COFFEE/MATTER FAMILY	
Galium circaezans	wild licorice	
Houstonia micrantha	southern bluets	C3
Hexasepalum teres	poorjoe	
RUTACEAE	CITRUS FAMILY	
Ptelea trifoliata	wafer ash/common hoptree	
SMILACACEAE	GREENBRIAR FAMILY	
Smilax spp		

SCIENTIFIC NAME	COMMON NAME	COEFFICIENT OF CONSERVATISM
SCROPHULARIACEAE	FIGWORT/SNAPDRAGON FAMILY	
Agalinis fasiculata	beach false foxglove	C3
Buchnera americana	American bluehearts	
Nuttallanthus texanus	Texas toadflax	C3
Pedicularis canadensis	lousewort	
Penstemon laxiflorus	nodding beardtongue	C8
SOLANACEAE	NIGHTSHADE/TOMATO FAMILY	
Solanum carolinense	Carolina horsenettle	C1
Physalis pubescens	groundcherry	
Physalis heterophylla	clammy groundcherry	
Solanum ptychanthum	Eastern black nightshade	
URTICACEAE	NETTLE FAMILY	
Boehmeria cylindrica	smallspike false nettle	C3
VERBENACEAE	VERVAIN FAMILY	
Verbena bonariensis	Brazilian vervain	nonnative
VIOLACEAE	VIOLET FAMILY	
Viola villosa	Carolina violet	
VITACEAE	GRAPE FAMILY	
Ampelopsis sp.	peppervine	C1
Parthenocissus quinquefolia	Virginia creeper	C2
Vitis rotundifolia	muscadine grape	
Vitis aestivalis	summer grape	

Note: C = species coefficient of conservatism in Louisiana coastal prairies (0–10)

Source: Larry Allain et al., "A Floristic Quality Assessment System for the Coastal Prairie of Louisiana," in *Proceedings of the 19th North American Prairie Conference,* ed. Dave Egan and John A. Harrington, 1–18 (Madison: University of Wisconsin–Madison, 2006). Most of the C-values were taken from this source. However, it should be noted that a few of the C-values listed in the Wafer Creek Ranch plants list came from botanists Latimore Smith and Chris Reid and are not in the original paper.

Notes

INTRODUCTION

1. Edward O. Wilson, "Fifty-Fifty: A Biologist's Manifesto for Preserving Life on Earth," *Sierra,* January/February 2017, digital.sierramagazine.org/publication/?m=43145&i=419589&p =30&pp=2&ver=htm15.

2. Wilson, "Fifty-Fifty."

WHY DOES OUR PLANET'S BIOSPHERE NEED TO BE RESCUED?

1. Frank White, *The Overview Effect* (Reston, VA: American Institute of Aeronautics and Astronautics, 1998).

2. Edward O. Wilson, *Half-Earth* (New York: Liveright, 2017).

3. "Why Are Amphibian Populations Declining?," US Geological Survey, https://www .usgs.gov/faqs/why-are-amphibian-populations-declining; P. J. Bishop et al., "The Amphibian Extinction Crisis—What Will It Take to Put the Action into the Amphibian Conservation Action Plan?," *Sapiens* 5, no. 2 (May 2012).

4. US Fish and Wildlife Service, "FEW-Listed US Species by Taxonomic Group—All Animals," Environmental Conservation Online System, https://ecos.fws.gov/ecp/report/species -listings-by-tax-group?statusCategory=Listed&groupName=All%20Animals.

5. Dimitry Wintermantel et al., "Field-level Clothianidin Exposure Affects Bumblebees but Generally Not Their Pathogens," *Nature Communications* 9, no. 1 (December 2018); Stephen Leahy, "Insect 'Apocalypse' in US Driven by 50x Increase in Toxic Pesticides," *National Geographic,* August 6, 2019.

6. Audubon, "Survival by Degrees: 389 Bird Species on the Brink," https://www.audubon .org/climate/survivalbydegrees; Cornell Lab of Ornithology, "Nearly 3 Billion Birds Gone Since 1970," https://www.birds.cornell.edu/home/bring-birds-back.

7. American Fisheries Society, "Imperiled Freshwater Organisms of North America Website," press release, January 12, 2014, https://fisheries.org/2014/01/imperiled-freshwater-organisms -of-north-america-website; "Recovering America's Wildlife Act Passes House," press release, June 14, 2022, https://fisheries.org/2022/06/recovering-americas-wildlife-act-passes-house.

8. World Wildlife Fund, "Sustainable Seafood, Overview," https://www.worldwildlife.org /industries/sustainable-seafood.

9. Rebecca Boehm, "Reviving the Dead Zone," Union of Concerned Scientists, June 1, 2020, https://www.ucsusa.org/resources/reviving-dead-zone.

10. Frank Kuznik, "America's Aching Mussels," *National Wildlife Federation,* November 1, 1993, https://www.nwf.org/Magazines/National-Wildlife/1993/America-s-Aching-Mussels.

11. Elizabeth Green et al., *Below the Canopy* (Washington, DC: World Wildlife Fund, 2019), https://files.worldwildlife.org/wwfcmsprod/files/Publication/file/41ubh70t7l_Below TheCanopy_Full_Report.pdf; Arie Rompas, "An Environmental Crisis in Borneo," Greenpeace, January 28, 2021, https://www.greenpeace.org/international/story/46328/environmental-crisis -borneo-flood-palm-oil-coal.

12. Elizabeth Kolbert, *The Sixth Extinction: An Unnatural History* (New York: Henry Holt, 2014); David Biello, "One Quarter of World's Mammals Face Extinction," *Scientific American,* October 6, 2008, https://www.scientificamerican.com/article/one-quarter-of-worlds -mammals-face-extinction.

13. Richard T. Corlett, "Plant Diversity in a Changing World: Status, Trends, and Conservation Needs," *Plant Diversity* 38, no. 1 (February 2016), 10–16.

14. Jennifer Skene and Shelley Vinyard, "The Issue with Tissue: How the US Is Flushing Forests Away," Natural Resources Defense Council, Expert Blog, February 20, 2019, https:// www.nrdc.org/experts/jennifer-skene/issue-tissue-how-us-flushing-forests-away; "24 Billion Tons of Fertile Land Lost Every Year, Warns UN Chief on World Day to Combat Desertification," United Nations, *UN News* June 16, 2019, https://news.un.org/en/story/2019/06/1040561; Rachel Ehrenberg, "Global Forest Survey Finds Trillions of Trees," *Nature,* September 2, 2015, https://doi.org/10.1038/nature.2015.18287.

15. Sara Tangren, "Native Plants and Climate Change," University of Maryland Extension, June 17, 2022, https://extension.umd.edu/resource/native-plants-and-climate-change.

16. Here I speak of today's version of an economy that is purely dollar oriented and not one concerned with our children's future. An economy based on the latter is green.

17. World Wildlife Fund, *Living Planet Report 2016: Risk and Resilience in a New Era* (Gland: WWF International, 2016), https://www.worldwildlife.org/pages/living-planet-report-2016; Nik Sekhran, "WWF's Nik Sekhran on the Push to Preserve the World's Biodiversity," World Wildlife Magazine, Fall 2018, https://www.worldwildlife.org/magazine/issues/fall-2018/articles /wwf-s-nik-sekhran-on-the-push-to-preserve-the-world-s-biodiversity.

18. Michael Greshko and National Geographic Staff, "What Are Mass Extinctions, and What Causes Them?," *National Geographic,* September 26, 2019, https://www.nationalgeographic.com /science/article/mass-extinction.

19. John Vidal, "Protect Nature for World Economic Security, Warns UN Biodiversity Chief," *Guardian,* August 16, 2010, https://www.theguardian.com/environment/2010/aug/16 /nature-economic-security.

20. Though I came up with this notion more than twenty years ago, there have been others who have also trod this ground, including a few writers, poets, artists, and scientists, who have explored and written about this subject for more than a century. In fact, E. O. Wilson has addressed this topic in at least two of his books, *Half-Earth* and *The Social Conquest of Earth.*

21. Michael Hopkin, "'Ruthlessness Gene' Discovered," *Nature,* April 4, 2008, https://www
.nature.com/articles/news.2008.738.

22. Carl Sagan, *Cosmos* (New York: Random House, 1980).

23. Kolbert, *Sixth Extinction.*

WHY SHOULD WE WORRY ABOUT "LITTLE SPECIES"?

1. Caspar Hallmann et al., "More than 75% Decline Over 27 Years in Total Flying Insect
Biomass in Protected Areas," *PLOS One,* October 18, 2017, https://doi.org/10.1371/journal.pone
.0185809.

2. Elizabeth Kolbert, "Where Have All the Insects Gone?," *National Geographic,* April 23,
2020, https://www.nationalgeographic.com/magazine/article/where-have-all-the-insects-gone
-feature.

3. Fred Krupp, "The Tipping Point," *Solutions* 52, no. 3 (Summer 2021): 3, https://www.edf
.org/sites/default/files/documents/solutions-Summer2021.pdf.

4. "All Creatures Great and Small," *Defenders Magazine,* Fall 2020, https://defenders.org
/magazine/fall-2020/all-creatures-great-and-small.

5. Sagan, *Cosmos.*

6. Leanna First-Arai, "The Sunrise Movement Comes to Nashville," *Sierra,* April 21, 2020,
sierraclub.org/sierra/2020-3-may-june/election-2020/sunrise-movement-comes-nashville.

MECHANISMS OF DESTRUCTION AND DEGRADATION
ON THE LOCAL LEVEL

1. Sam Davis, "Why Is Biomass Bad: 5 Reasons Why the World Must Stop Importing Bioenergy," Dogwood Alliance, March 15, 2022, https://www.dogwoodalliance.org/2022/03/5
-reasons-why-the-world-must-stop-importing-bioenergy.

2. Roger Drouin, "Wood Pellets: Green Energy or New Source of CO_2 Emissions?," *Yale
Environment 360,* January 22, 2015, https://e360.yale.edu/features/wood_pellets_green_energy
_or_new_source_of_co2_emissions.

3. "Climate Impact of Woody Biomass," European Academies Science Advisory Council, press
release, January 27, 2021, https://easac.eu/media-room/press-releases/details/easac-welcomes
-that-the-jrc-report-strengthens-the-case-for-shorter-payback-periods-on-woody-biomass.

4. Citi Group, December 2, 2021, in Davis, "Why Is Biomass Bad."

5. Matt Lee-Ashley et al., "How Much Nature Should America Keep?," Center for American Progress, August 9, 2019, https://www.americanprogress.org/article/much-nature
-america-keep.

6. Tom Springer, "30 x 30: Putting Private Land Conservation on the Map, *Saving Land
Magazine,* Summer 2021, https://www.landtrustalliance.org/news/30x30-putting-private-land
-conservation-map; "1st Draft of The Post-2020 Global Biodiversity Framework," United Nations Environment Programme, July 12, 2021, https://www.unep.org/resources/publication
/1st-draft-post-2020-global-biodiversity-framework.

RESTORATION ECOLOGY OF THE
SHORTLEAF PINE-OAK-HICKORY WOODLAND

1. Edward O. Wilson, *The Diversity of Life* (Cambridge, MA: Belknap Press of Harvard University Press, 1992).

2. Robert MacArthur and Edward O. Wilson, *The Theory of Island Biogeography* (Princeton, NJ: Princeton University Press, 1967).

3. Kolbert, Sixth Extinction.

4. Darwin Spearing, *Roadside Geology of Louisiana,* 2nd ed. (Missoula, MT: Mountain Press, 2007); Kolbert, *Sixth Extinction.*

5. Chris Reid and Amity Bass, "Prairie in Louisiana," *Louisiana Wildlife Insider,* Winter 2014, https://www.wlf.louisiana.gov/assets/Resources/Publications/Wildlife_Insider/2014 _Winter_Wildlife_Insider.pdf.

6. Joseph H. Williams, "Tallgrass Prairie Reserve," Nature Conservancy, July 2014, nature .org/content/dam/tnc/nature/en/documents/TGP-Brochure-1.pdf; Robert E. Howells, "This Is One of the Last Remnants of American Prairie," *National Geographic,* March 26, 2020, national geographic.com/travel/article/discover-american-landscape-in-tallgrass-prairie-preserve.

7. Reed F. Noss, Forgotten Grasslands of the South: Natural History and Conservation (Washington, DC: Island Press, 2013), 2.

SALIENT WARM SEASON GRASSES OF THE
WOODLAND GROUNDCOVER

1. Per-Olav Moksnes et al., "Major Impacts and Societal Costs of Seagrass Loss on Sediment Carbon and Nitrogen Stocks," *Ecosphere,* July 29, 2021, https://doi.org/10.1002/ecs2.3658.

2. J. Loisel, et al., "Expert Assessment of Future Vulnerability of the Global Peatland Carbon Sink," *Nature Climate Change,* 2021, nps.gov/articles/000/peatlands.htm. The International Peatland Society (peatlands.org) is also a source to learn about peatlands and peatland restoration.

3. Kat Kerlin, "Grasslands More Reliable Carbon Sink Than Trees," UC Davis, July 9, 2018, climatechange.ucdavis.edu/news/grasslands-more-reliable-carbon-sink-than-trees; Ashley Ahearn, "Carbon-Offset Cowboys Let Their Grass Grow," *Scientific American,* December 1, 2008, https://www.scientificamerican.com/article/carbon-cowboys.

4. "Fires conducted in late spring and early summer are especially effective inducers of bloom and seed production in warm season grasses." Latimore Smith, pers. comm.

5. North Carolina Extension (NCE) Gardener Plant Toolbox, "*Schizachyrium scoparium*" [little bluestem], https://plants.ces.ncsu.edu/plants/schizachyrium-scoparium; Illinois Wildflowers, "Little Bluestem, *Schizachyrium scoparium,*" https://illinoiswildflowers.info/grasses /plants/little_bluestem.htm.

6. United States Department of Agriculture (USDA) Natural Resources Conservation Service (NRCS), Plants database, "*Aristida purpurascens* Poir. arrowfeather threeawn," https://plants .usda.gov/home/plantProfile?symbol=ARPU8.

7. Melanie J. Kaeser and L. Katherine Kirkman, *Field and Restoration Guide to Common Native Warm-Season Grasses of the Longleaf Pine Ecosystem* (Newton, GA: Joseph W. Jones Ecological Research Center, 2020). https://www.nclongleaf.org/pdfs/FieldGuideGrasses_Jones Center.pdf.

8. USDA NRCS Plants database, "*Andropogon ternarius* Michx., splitbeard bluestem," https://plants.usda.gov/home/plantProfile?symbol=ANTE2.

9. NCE Gardener Plant Toolbox, "*Andropogon ternarius*" [bluestem], https://plants.ces.ncsu.edu/plants/andropogon-ternarius.

10. USDA and US Forest Service Fire Effects Information System (FEIS), "Index of Species Information," "*Andropogon ternarius* var. *cabanisii*," https://www.fs.fed.us/database/feis/plants/graminoid/andterc/all.html.

11. Michigan State University Extension, Michigan Natural Features Inventory, "*Sporobolus clandestinus*, dropseed," https://mnfi.anr.msu.edu/species/description/15778/Sporobolus%20clandestinus; USDA NRCS Plants database, "*Sporobolus clandestinus* (Biehler) Hitchc., rough dropseed," https://plants.usda.gov/home/plantProfile?symbol=SPCL.

12. Lady Bird Johnson (LBJ) Wildflower Center, Plant Database, "*Andropogon gerardii*," https://www.wildflower.org/plants/result.php?id_plant=ANGE.

13. USDA NRCS Plants database, "*Andropogon gerardii* Vitman, big bluestem," https://plants.usda.gov/home/plantProfile?symbol=ANGE.

14. USDA NRCS Plants database, "*Andropogon gyrans* Ashe, Elliott's bluestem," https://plants.usda.gov/home/plantProfile?symbol=ANGY2.

15. USDA NRCS Plants database, "*Sorghastrum elliottii* (C. Mohr) Nash, slender Indiangrass," https://plants.usda.gov/home/plantProfile?symbol=SOEL3.

16. LBJ Wildflower Center, Plant Database, "*Eragrostis spectabilis*," https://www.wildflower.org/plants/result.php?id_plant=ERSP.

17. Missouri Botanical Garden (MoBG), Plant Finder, "*Eragrostis spectabilis*," https://www.missouribotanicalgarden.org/PlantFinder/PlantFinderDetails.aspx?taxonid=285200&isprofile=1&basic=Eragrostis%20spectabilis.

18. NCE Gardener Plant Toolbox, "*Eragrostis spectabilis*" [purple lovegrass] https://plants.ces.ncsu.edu/plants/eragrostis-spectabilis.

19. Illinois Wildflowers, "Purple Love Grass, *Eragrostis spectabilis*," https://illinoiswildflowers.info/grasses/plants/pp_lovegrass.htm.

20. *Saccharum brevibarbe*, Flora of North America, http://floranorthamerica.org/Saccharum_brevibarbe; Allen Weakley and the Southeastern Flora Team, *Flora of the Southeastern United States: Louisiana*, North Carolina Botanical Garden, University of North Carolina at Chapel Hill Herbarium (2022), https://fsus.ncbg.unc.edu/img/flora/FSUS2022_Louisiana.pdf

21. USDA NRCS Plants database, "*Saccharum brevibarbe* (Michx.) *Pers. var. contortum* (Elliott) R. Webster, sortbeard plumegrass," https://plants.usda.gov/home/plantProfile?symbol=SABRC3.

22. NCE Gardener Plant Toolbox, "*Saccharum giganteum*" [giant plumegrass], https://plants.ces.ncsu.edu/plants/saccharum-giganteum.

23. Field identification by Latimore Smith, Southern Wild Heritage.

24. MoBG, Plant Finder, "*Muhlenbergia capillaris,*" https://www.missouribotanicalgarden .org/PlantFinder/PlantFinderComments.aspx?kempercode=b457; USDA NRCS Plants database, "*Muhlenbergia capillaris* (Lam.) Trin., hairawn muhly," https://plants.usda.gov/home /plantProfile?symbol=MUCA2; LBJ Wildflower Center, Plant Database, "*Muhlenbergia capillaris,*" https://www.wildflower.org/plants/result.php?id_plant=MUCA2.

25. NCE Gardener Plant Toolbox, "*Muhlenbergia capillaris*" [Gulf muhly], https://plants.ces .ncsu.edu/plants/muhlenbergia-capillaris.

26. USDA NRCS Plants database, "*Panicum anceps* Michx., beaked panicgrass," https:// plants.usda.gov/home/plantProfile?symbol=PAAN.

27. LBJ Wildflower Center, Plant Database, "*Tridens flavus var. flavus,*" https://www.wildflower .org/plants/result.php?id_plant=TRFLF.

28. USDA NRCS Plants database, "*Tridens flavus* (L.) Hitchc., purpletop tridens," https:// plants.usda.gov/home/plantProfile?symbol=TRFL2.

29. LBJ Wildflower Center, Plant Database, "*Aristida oligantha,*" https://www.wildflower .org/plants/result.php?id_plant=AROL.

30. Illinois Wildflowers, "Prairie Three-Awn, *Aristida oligantha,*" illinoiswildflowers.info /grasses/plants/pr_3awn.htm.

31. USDA NRCS Plants database, "*Andropogon virginicus* L., broomsedge bluestem," https:// plants.usda.gov/home/plantProfile?symbol=ANVI2.

32. LBJ Wildflower Center, Plant Database, "*Andropogon glomeratus,*" https://www.wildflower .org/plants/result.php?id_plant=ANGL2; NCE Gardener Plant Toolbox, "*Andropogon glomeratus*" [bushy bluestem], https://plants.ces.ncsu.edu/plants/andropogon-glomeratus.

33. LBJ Wildflower Center, Plant Database, "*Andropogon glomeratus*"; USDA NRCS Plants database, "*Andropogon glomeratus* (Walter) Britton, Sterns & Poggenb., bushy bluestem," https:// plants.usda.gov/home/plantProfile?symbol=ANGL2.

34. USDA NRCS Plants database, "*Chasmanthium laxum* (L.) Yates, slender woodoats," https://plants.usda.gov/home/plantProfile?symbol=CHLA6.

35. Coastal Plain Plants wiki, "*Chasmanthium laxum,*" http://coastalplainplants.org/wiki /index.php/Chasmanthium_laxum.

36. Coastal Plain Plants wiki, "*Dichanthelium_scoparium,*" http://coastalplainplants.org/wiki /index.php/Dichanthelium_scoparium.

FORBS AND OTHER NONGRASS SPECIES OF THE SHORTLEAF PINE-OAK-HICKORY WOODLAND GROUNDCOVER

1. MoBG, Plant Finder, "*Manfreda virginica,*" https://www.missouribotanicalgarden.org/Plant Finder/PlantFinderDetails.aspx?taxonid=275823.

2. USDA NRCS Plants database, "*Manfreda virginica* (L.) Salisb. ex Rose, false aloe," https:// plants.usda.gov/home/plantProfile?symbol=MAVI5.

3. Illinois Wildflowers, "Eastern Agave, *Manfreda virginica,*" illinoiswildflowers.info/savanna /plants/east_agave.html.

4. Latimore Smith, pers. comm.

5. USDA NRCS Plants database, "*Yucca filamentosa* L., Adam's needle," https://plants.usda.gov/home/plantProfile?symbol=YUFI.

LBJ Wildflower Center, Plant Database, "*Yucca filamentosa*," https://www.wildflower.org/plants/result.php?id_plant=YUFI.

6. Florida Native Plant Society (FNPS), "*Yucca filamentosa*," https://www.fnps.org/plant/yucca-filamentosa.

7. Virginia Native Plant Society, "2008 Virginia Spiderwort (*Tradescantia virginiana*)," https://vnps.org/2008-virginia-spiderwort-tradescantia-virginiana.

8. Illinois Wildflowers, "Virginia Spiderwort, *Tradescantia virginiana*," https://illinois wildflowers.info/savanna/plants/va_spiderwort.htm.

9. LBJ Wildflower Center, Plant Database, "*Tradescantia virginiana*," https://www.wildflower.org/plants/result.php?id_plant=TRVI.

10. S. Nicole Frey and Heather Heaton, "Using Plants to Attract Hummingbirds to Your Yard," Natural Resources Extension, Utah State University, July 2013, https://digitalcommons.usu.edu/cgi/viewcontent.cgi?article=2253&context=extension_curall.

11. Illinois Wildflowers, "Wild Bergamot, *Monarda fistulosa*," illinoiswildflowers.info/prairie/plantx/wld_bergamotx.htm.

12. USDA NRCS Plants database, "*Monarda punctata* L., spotted beebalm," https://plants.usda.gov/home/plantProfile?symbol=MOPU.

13. USDA NRCS Plants database, "*Salvia azurea* Michx. ex Lam., azure blue sage," https://plants.usda.gov/home/plantProfile?symbol=SAAZ.

14. Flowers by the Sea, "*Salvia azurea*," https://www.fbts.com/salvia-azurea.html?utm_source=search&utm_medium=site_search&utm_campaign=1157:1; Illinois Wildflowers, "Wild Blue Sage, *Salvia azurea grandiflora*," illinoiswildflowers.info/prairie/plantx/blue_sagex.htm.

15. USDA NRCS Plants database, "*Pycnanthemum albescens* Torr. & A. Gray, whiteleaf mountainmint," https://plants.usda.gov/home/plantProfile?symbol=PYAL.

16. LBJ Wildflower Center, Plant Database, "*Pycnanthemum tenuifolium*," https://www.wildflower.org/plants/result.php?id_plant=PYTE.

17. USDA NRCS Plants database, "*Pycnanthemum tenuifolium* Schrad., narrowleaf mountainmint," https://plants.usda.gov/home/plantProfile?symbol=PYTE.

18. USDA NRCS Plants database, "*Trichostema dichotomum* L., forked bluecurls," https://plants.usda.gov/home/plantProfile?symbol=TRDI2.

19. FNPS, "*Trichostema dichotomum*," https://www.fnps.org/plant/trichostema-dichotomum.

20. bplant.org, "rattlesnake master (*Eryngium yuccifolium* Michx.)," https://bplant.org/plant/2752.

21. Eric Ulaszek and Christopher David Benda, "Plant of the Week: Rattlesnake Master (*Eryngium yuccifolium* L.)," US Forest Service, https://www.fs.fed.us/wildflowers/plant-of-the-week/Eryngium-yuccifolium.shtml.

22. FNPS, "*Erythrina herbacea*," https://www.fnps.org/plant/erythrina-herbacea.

23. USDA NRCS Plants database, "*Desmodium rotundifolium* DC., prostrate ticktrefoil," https://plants.usda.gov/home/plantProfile?symbol=DERO3.

24. Ozark Edge Wildflowers, "Dollar-leaf, *Desmodium rotundifolium*," ozarkedgewildflowers.com/summer-wildflowers/dollar-leaf-desmodium-rotundifolium.

25. Larry Allain, USGS, "*Lespedeza hirta,* hairy lespedeza, hairy bush clover," Plants of Louisiana, https://warcapps.usgs.gov/PlantID/Species/Details/1144.

26. USDA NRCS Plants database, "*Lespedeza hirta* (L.) Hornem., hairy lespedeza," https://plants.usda.gov/home/plantProfile?symbol=LEHI2.

27. Illinois Wildflowers, "Hairy Bush Clover, *Lespedeza hirta,*" illinoiswildflowers.info/savanna/plants/hry_bushclover.htm.

28. Illinois Wildflowers, "Slender Bush Clover, *Lespedeza virginica,*" illinoiswildflowers.info/savanna/plants/sl_bushclover.htm; NCE Gardener Plant Toolbox, "*Lespedeza virginica*" [bush clover], https://plants.ces.ncsu.edu/plants/lespedeza-virginica.

29. USDA NRCS Plants database, "*Lespedeza virginica* (L.) Britton, slender lespedeza," https://plants.usda.gov/home/plantProfile?symbol=LEVI7.

30. USDA NRCS Plants database, "*Strophostyles umbellata* (Muhl. ex Willd.) Britton, pink fuzzybean," https://plants.usda.gov/home/plantProfile?symbol=STUM2; Coastal Plain Plants wiki, "*Strophostyles umbellata,*" coastalplainplants.org/wiki/index.php/Strophostyles_umbellata.

31. USDA NRCS Plants database, "*Chamaecrista fasciculata* (Michx.) Greene, partridge pea," https://plants.usda.gov/home/plantProfile?symbol=CHFA2.

32. Illinois Wildflowers, "Partridge Pea, *Chamaecrista fasciculata,*" illinoiswildflowers.info/prairie/plantx/part_peax.htm.

33. USDA NRCS Plants database, "*Centrosema virginianum* (L.) Benth., spurred butterfly pea," https://plants.usda.gov/home/plantProfile?symbol=CEVI2; Institute for Regional Conservation, "Spurred butterfly-pea, *Centrosema virginianum,*" regionalconservation.org/beta/nfyn/plantdetail.asp?tx=centvirg&tx=centvirg.

34. USDA NRCS Plants database, "*Mimosa nuttallii* (DC. ex Britton & Rose) B.L. Turner, Nuttall's sensitive-briar," https://plants.usda.gov/home/plantProfile?symbol=MINU6.

35. Ozark Edge Wildflowers, "Sensitive brier (*Mimosa nuttallii*)," https://ozarkedgewildflowers.com/summer-wildflowers/sensitive-brier-mimosa-nuttallii.

36. USDA NRCS Plants database, "*Tephrosia virginiana* (L.) Pers., Virginia tephrosia," https://plants.usda.gov/home/plantProfile?symbol=TEVI.

37. Illinois Wildflowers, "Goat's Rue, *Tephrosia virginiana,*" illinoiswildflowers.info/prairie/plantx/goat_rue.htm.

38. USDA NRCS Plants database, "*Rhynchosia tomentosa* (L.) Hook. & Arn., twining snoutbean," https://plants.usda.gov/home/plantProfile?symbol=RHTO3.

39. USDA NRCS Plants database, "*Rhynchosia latifolia* Nutt. ex Torr. & A. Gray, prairie snoutbean," https://plants.usda.gov/home/plantProfile?symbol=RHLA5.

40. NCE Gardener Plant Toolbox, "*Stylosanthes biflora*" [pencil flower], plants.ces.ncsu.edu/plants/stylosanthes-biflora.

41. Illinois Wildflowers, "Pencil Flower, *Stylosanthes biflora,*" illinoiswildflowers.info/savanna/plants/pencil_flw.html.

42. USDA NRCS Plants database, "*Stylosanthes biflora* (L.) Britton, Sterns & Poggenb.," sidebeak pencilflower," https://plants.usda.gov/home/plantProfile?symbol=STBI2.

43. USDA NRCS Plants database, "*Galactia volubilis* (L.) Britton, downy milkpea," https://plants.usda.gov/home/plantProfile?symbol=GAVO; Coastal Plain Plants wiki, "*Galactia volubilis*," coastalplainplants.org/wiki/index.php/Galactia_volubilis.

44. University of Wisconsin–Madison, Wisconsin Horticulture, Division of Extension, "Common Milkweed Insects," https://hort.extension.wisc.edu/articles/common-milkweed-insects.

45. USDA NRCS Plants database, "*Asclepias variegata* L., redring milkweed," https://plants.usda.gov/home/plantProfile?symbol=ASVA; "*Asclepias amplexicaulis* Sm., clasping milkweed," https://plants.usda.gov/home/plantProfile?symbol=ASAM; "*Asclepias tuberosa* L., butterfly milkweed," https://plants.usda.gov/home/plantProfile?symbol=ASTU.

46. Chris Doffitt, botanist, Louisiana Department of Wildlife and Fisheries, pers. comm.

47. USDA NRCS Plants database, "*Matelea gonocarpos* (Walter) Shinners, angularfruit milkvine," https://plants.usda.gov/home/plantProfile?symbol=MAGO.

48. Sid Vogelpohl, "Know Your Natives—Baldwin's Climbing Milkweed and Anglepod Milkvine," Arkansas Native Plant Society, October 26, 2014, https://anps.org/2014/10/26/know-your-natives-baldwins-climbing-milkweed-and-anglepod-milkvine.

49. Ozark Edge Wildflowers, "Climbing Milkweed (*Matelea Decipiens*)," https://ozarkedgewildflowers.com/climbing-milkweed-matelea-decipiens.

50. USDA NRCS Plants database, "*Euphorbia corollata* L., flowering spurge," https://plants.usda.gov/home/plantProfile?symbol=EUCO10; Illinois Wildflowers, "Flowering Spurge, *Euphorbia corollata*," http://www.illinoiswildflowers.info/prairie/plantx/flw_spurgex.htm.

51. USDA NRCS Plants database, "*Tragia urticifolia* Michx., nettleleaf noseburn," https://plants.usda.gov/home/plantProfile?symbol=TRUR2.

52. Latimore Smith, pers. comm.

53. Mark Vorderbruggen, "Bull Nettle," *Foraging Texas,* https://www.foragingtexas.com/2008/07/bull-nettle.html.

54. LBJ Wildflower Center, Plant Database, "*Croton capitatus*," https://www.wildflower.org/plants/result.php?id_plant=CRCA6; NCE Gardener Plant Toolbox, "*Croton capitatus*" [hogwort], https://plants.ces.ncsu.edu/plants/croton-capitatus.

55. USDA NRCS Plants database, "*Croton capitatus* Michx., hogwort," https://plants.usda.gov/home/plantProfile?symbol=CRCA6.

56. Illinois Wildflowers, "Sand Croton, *Croton glandulosus septentrionalis*," https://illinoiswildflowers.info/prairie/plantx/sand_croton.html.

57. David Moreland, "Checklist of Woody and Herbaceous Deer Food Plants of Louisiana," Louisiana Department of Wildlife and Fisheries, Wildlife Division, 2005.

58. USDA NRCS Plants database, "*Croton glandulosus* L., vente conmigo," https://plants.usda.gov/home/plantProfile?symbol=CRGL2.

59. USDA NRCS Plants database, "*Acalypha gracilens* A. Gray, slender threeseed mercury," https://plants.usda.gov/home/plantProfile?symbol=ACGR2.

60. Coastal Plain Plants wiki, "*Acalypha Gracilens*," coastalplainplants.org/wiki/index.php/Acalypha_gracilens.

61. Royal Botanic Gardens, Kew, "*Hypericum hypericoides* subsp. *Hypericoides,*" Plants of the World Online, powo.science.kew.org/taxon/urn:lsid:ipni.org:names:77173319-1.

62. FNPS, "*Hypericum hypericoides,*" https://www.fnps.org/plant/hypericum-hypericoides; Florida Wildflower Foundation, "St. Andrew's cross," https://www.flawildflowers.org/flower-friday-hypericum-hypericoides; NCE Gardener Plant Toolbox, "*Hypericum hypericoides subsp. Multicaule*" [decumbent St. Andrews cross], https://plants.ces.ncsu.edu/plants/hypericum-hypericoides-subsp-multicaule.

63. Identification thanks to Chris Reid, botanist, Louisiana State University, pers. comm.

64. Illinois Wildflowers, "Wafer Ash, *Ptelea trifoliata,*" illinoiswildflowers.info/trees/plants/wafer_ash.htm; LBJ Wildflower Center, Plant Database, "*Ptelea trifoliata,*" https://www.wildflower.org/plants/result.php?id_plant=PTTR.

65. LBJ Wildflower Center, Plant Database, "Plant Family: *Melastomataceae,*" https://www.wildflower.org/plants/search.php?search_field=&family=Melastomataceae&newsearch=true&demo=.

66. USDA NRCS Plants database, "*Rhexia mariana* L., Maryland meadowbeauty," https://plants.usda.gov/home/plantProfile?symbol=RHMA.

67. Missouri Wildflowers Nursery, "Meadow Beauty (*Rhexia mariana var. interior*)," mowildflowers-net.3dcartstores.com/Meadow-Beauty-Rhexia-mariana-var-interior_p_221.html.

68. Illinois Wildflowers, "Virgin's Bower, *Clematis virginiana,*" illinoiswildflowers.info/savanna/plants/virgin_bower.htm.

69. USDA NRCS Plants database, "*Clematis virginiana* L., devil's darning needles," https://plants.usda.gov/home/plantProfile?symbol=CLVI5.

70. Illinois Wildflowers, "Common Rose Pink, *Sabatia angularis,*" illinoiswildflowers.info/prairie/plantx/cm_rosepink.htm.

71. USDA NRCS Plants database, "*Oenothera lindheimeri* (Engelm. & A. Gray) W.L. Wagner & Hoch, Lindheimer's beeblossom," https://plants.usda.gov/home/plantProfile?symbol=OELI2; LBJ Wildflower Center, Plant Database, "*Oenothera lindheimeri,*" https://www.wildflower.org/plants/result.php?id_plant=OELI2.

72. NCE Gardener Plant Toolbox, "*Oenothera lindheimeri*" [Indian feather, Lindheimer's clockweed, pink gaura, whirling butterflies, white gaura], https://plants.ces.ncsu.edu/plants/oenothera-lindheimeri.

73. Mark Vorderbruggen, "Common Evening Primrose," *Foraging Texas,* https://www.foragingtexas.com/search?q=Common+Evening+Primrose; LBJ Wildflower Center, Plant Database, "*Oenothera biennis,*" https://www.wildflower.org/plants/result.php?id_plant=OEBI.

74. USDA NRCS Plants database, "*Oenothera biennis* L., common evening primrose," https://plants.usda.gov/home/plantProfile?symbol=OEBI.

75. Illinois Wildflowers, "Wild Sweet Potato, *Ipomoea pandurata,*" illinoiswildflowers.info/savanna/plants/ws_potato.htm.

76. NCE Gardener Plant Toolbox, "*Ipomoea pandurata*" [Indian potato], https://plants.ces.ncsu.edu/plants/ipomoea-pandurata.

77. Illinois Wildflowers, "Wild Sweet Potato."

78. USDA NRCS Plants database, "*Ipomoea pandurata* (L.) G. Mey., man of the earth," https://plants.usda.gov/home/plantProfile?symbol=IPPA.

79. Alabamaplants.com, "*Jacquemontia tamnifolia* (L.) Griseb.—Hairy Clustervine," alabama plants.com/Bluealt/Jacquemontia_tamnifolia_page.html; Center for Invasive Species and Ecosystem Health, "*Jacquemontia tamnifolia*," https://www.invasive.org/browse/subinfo.cfm?sub=5798.

80. USDA NRCS Plants database, "*Ipomoea cordatotriloba* Dennst., tievine," https://plants .usda.gov/home/plantProfile?symbol=IPC08; Wild South Florida, "Tievine, *Ipomoea cordatotriloba*," http://wildsouthflorida.com/tievine.html#.YsyDGXbMKUl.

81. Coastal Plain Plants wiki, "*Ipomoea cordotriloba*," http://coastalplainplants.org/wiki/index .php/Ipomoea_cordatotriloba.

82. USDA NRCS Plants database, "*Solanum carolinense* L., Carolina horsenettle," https:// plants.usda.gov/home/plantProfile?symbol=SOCA3; Illinois Wildflowers, "Horse Nettle, *Solanum carolinense*," illinoiswildflowers.info/prairie/plantx/hrs_nettlex.htm.

83. Britannica, "Bluebell," britannica.com/plant/bluebell-plant-genus-Hyacinthoides.

84. Thomas G. Lammers, "Revision of the Endemic Hawaiian genus *Trematolobelia* (*Campanulaceae: Lobelioideae*)," *Brittonia* (June 1, 2009), 126–143.

85. USDA NRCS Plants database, "*Lobelia appendiculata* A. DC., pale lobelia," https:// plants.usda.gov/home/plantProfile?symbol=SOCA3.

86. Larry Allain, USGS, "*Lobelia appendiculata,* pale lobelia, earflower lobelia," Plants of Louisiana, warcapps.usgs.gov/PlantID/Species/Details/1623.

87. Betsy Washington, "Downy Lobelia: An Overlooked Garden Native," Virginia Native Plant Society, January 7, 2020, vnps.org/downy-lobelia-an-overlooked-garden-native.

88. USDA NRCS Plants database, "*Lobelia puberula* Michx., downy lobelia," https://plants .usda.gov/home/plantProfile?symbol=LOPU.

89. LBJ Wildflower Center, Plant Database, "*Lobelia cardinalis,*" https://www.wildflower .org/plants/result.php?id_plant=loca2.

90. Calscape, "Cardinal Flower, *Lobelia cardinalis var. pseudosplendens,*" California Native Plant Society, https://calscape.org/loc-California/Cardinal%20Flower,%20Lobelia%20 cardinalis(%20).

91. Calscape, "Clasping Venus' Looking Glass, *Triodanis perfoliata,*" California Native Plant Society, calscape.org/loc-California/Clasping%20Venus'%20Looking-glass%20 (Triodanis%20 perfoliata).

92. Illinois Wildflowers, "Venus' Looking Glass," illinoiswildflowers.info/prairie/plantx /venusx.htm.

93. BioNinja, "Reclassification of Figworts (Family *Scrophulariaceae*)," ib.bioninja.com.au /standard-level/topic-5-evolution-and-biodi/54-cladistics/clade-reclassification.html.

94. USDA NRCS Plants database, "*Penstemon laxiflorus* Pennell, nodding beardtongue," https://plants.usda.gov/home/plantProfile?symbol=PELA10.

95. LBJ Wildflower Center, Plant Database, "*Penstemon laxiflorus,*" https://www.wildflower .org/plants/result.php?id_plant=PELA10.

96. USDA NRCS Plants database, "*Nuttallanthus texanus* (Scheele) D.A. Sutton, Texas toadflax," https://plants.usda.gov/home/plantProfile?symbol=NUTE.

97. North American Butterfly Association, "Texas Toadflax (*Nuttallanthus texanus*)," https:// nababutterfly.com/texas-toadflax.

98. Britannica, "*Orobanchaceae*," https://www.britannica.com/plant/Lamiales/Orobancha ceae.

99. Missouri Plants, "*Agalinis fasciculata* (Elliott) Raf.," missouriplants.com/Agalinis _fasciculata_page.html; USDA NRCS Plants database, "*Agalinis fasciculata* (Elliott) Raf.," https:// plants.usda.gov/home/plantProfile?symbol=AGFA2.

100. Coastal Plain Plants wiki, "*Agalinis fasciculata*," coastalplainplants.org/wiki/index.php /Agalinis_fasciculata.

101. USDA NRCS Plants database, "*Polygala polygama,* Racemed Milkwort," https://plants .usda.gov/home/plantProfile?symbol=POPO.

102. Minnesota Wildflowers, "*Polygala polygama* (Racemed Milkwort)," minnesotawild flowers.info/flower/racemed-milkwort.

103. Illinois Wildflowers, "Purple Milkwort, *Polygala polygama,*" illinoiswildflowers.info /savanna/plants/pp_milkwort.html.

104. Patrick Catling, "Pollination of Northeastern North American *Spiranthes* (*Orchidaceae*)," *Canadian Journal of Botany,* April 1, 1983.

105. North American Orchid Conservation Center, "*Tipularia discolor* (Pursh) Nutt., Crane- fly Orchid," https://goorchids.northamericanorchidcenter.org/species/tipularia/discolor; "The Cranefly Orchid (*Tipularia discolor*)," *In Defense of Plants,* July 20, 2016, https://www.indefense ofplants.com/blog/2016/7/20/the-cranefly-orchid-tipularia-discolor.

106. USDA NRCS Plants database, "*Tipularia discolor* (Pursh) Nutt., crippled cranefly," https://plants.usda.gov/home/plantProfile?symbol=TIDI.

107. Rupesh Paudyal, "*Monotropa uniflora:* How a Plant Conned Fungi," TalkPlant blog, May 27, 2017, www.talkplant.com/real-hustle-plant-conned-fungi.

108. Illinois Wildflowers, "Indian Pipe, *Monotropa uniflora,*" illinoiswildflowers.info/wood land/plants/indian_pipe.htm.

109. Clair A. Brown, *Wildflowers of Louisiana and Adjoining States,* Baton Rouge: Louisiana State University Press, 1980); LBJ Wildflower Center, Plant Database, "*Monotropa uniflora,*" https://www.wildflower.org/plants/result.php?id_plant=MOUN3.

110. NCE Gardener Plant Toolbox, "*Passiflora lutea*" [dwarf passionflower, eastern yellow passionflower, hardy yellow passionflower, passion flower], https://plants.ces.ncsu.edu/plants /passiflora-lutea.

111. NCE Gardener Plant Toolbox, "*Passiflora incarnata*" [apricot vine, maypop, passion- flower, passion flower, passion vine], https://plants.ces.ncsu.edu/plants/passiflora-incarnata.

112. "Flowers of the Day: Sunflowers," *Elizabeth's Wildflower Blog,* August 19, 2014, https:// elizabethswildflowerblog.com/2014/08/19/flowers-of-the-day-sunflowers.

113. USDA NRCS Plants database, "*Packera tomentosa* (Michx.) C. Jeffrey, woolly ragwort," https://plants.usda.gov/home/plantProfile?symbol=PATo4.

114. USDA NRCS Plants database, "*Rudbeckia hirta* L., blackeyed Susan," https://plants .usda.gov/home/plantProfile?symbol=RUHI2.

115. LBJ Wildflower Center, Plant Database, "*Rudbeckia hirta,*" https://www.wildflower.org/plants/result.php?id_plant=RUHI2.

116. bplant.org, "rough coneflower (*Rudbeckia grandiflora* (D. Don) J.F. Gmel. ex DC)," https://bplant.org/plant/3201.

117. LBJ Wildflower Center, Plant Database, "*Rudbeckia grandiflora,*" https://www.wildflower.org/plants/result.php?id_plant=RUGR.

118. Larry Allain, USGS, "*Rudbeckia grandiflora,* tall coneflower, rough coneflower, plantainleaf coneflower," Plants of Louisiana, https://warcapps.usgs.gov/PlantID/Species/Details/2221.

119. USDA NRCS Plants database, "*Pluchea camphorata* (L.) DC., camphor pluchea," https://plants.usda.gov/home/plantProfile?symbol=PLCA7.

120. Illinois Wildflowers, "Camphorweed, *Heterotheca subaxillaris latifolia,*" illinoiswildflowers.info/prairie/plantx/camphorweed.html.

121. USDA NRCS Plants database, "*Heterotheca subaxillaris* (Lam.) Britton & Rusby, camphorweed," https://plants.usda.gov/home/plantProfile?symbol=HESU3; Calscape, "Camphorweed, *Heterotheca subaxillaris,*" California Native Plant Society, https://calscape.org/loc-California/Heterotheca%20subaxillaris%20(Camphorweed).

122. Illinois Wildflowers, "Yellow Crownbeard, *Verbesina helianthoides,*" illinoiswildflowers.info/prairie/plantx/crownbeardx.htm.

123. USDA NRCS Plants database, "*Verbesina helianthoides* Michx., gravelweed," https://plants.usda.gov/home/plantProfile?symbol=VEHE.

124. USDA NRCS Plants database, "*Euthamia leptocephala* (Torr. & A. Gray) Greene ex Porter & Britton, bushy goldentop," https://plants.usda.gov/home/plantProfile?symbol=EULE4.

125. LBJ Wildflower Center, Plant Database, "*Euthamia leptocephala,*" https://www.wildflower.org/plants/result.php?id_plant=EULE4.

126. LBJ Wildflower Center, Plant Database, "*Eupatorium rotundifolium,*" https://www.wildflower.org/plants/result.php?id_plant=EURO4.

127. USDA NRCS Plants database, "*Eupatorium rotundifolium* L., roundleaf thoroughwort," https://plants.usda.gov/home/plantProfile?symbol=EURO4.

128. LBJ Wildflower Center, Plant Database, "*Eupatorium album,*" https://www.wildflower.org/plants/result.php?id_plant=EUAL2.

129. Illinois Wildflowers, "Common Boneset, *Eupatorium perfoliatum,*" illinoiswildflowers.info/prairie/plantx/cm_boneset.htm.

130. LBJ Wildflower Center, Plant Database, "*Eupatorium perfoliatum,*" https://www.wildflower.org/plants/result.php?id_plant=EUPE3.

131. LBJ Wildflower Center, Plant Database, "*Eupatorium serotinum,*" https://www.wildflower.org/plants/result.php?id_plant=EUSE2.

132. Illinois Wildflowers, "Late Boneset, *Eupatorium serotinum,*" illinoiswildflowers.info/prairie/plantx/late_bonesetx.htm.

133. USDA NRCS Plants database, "*Eupatorium serotinum* Michx., lateflowering thoroughwort," https://plants.usda.gov/home/plantProfile?symbol=EUSE2.

134. MoBG, Plant Finder, *"Symphyotrichum patens,"* https://www.missouribotanical garden.org/PlantFinder/PlantFinderDetails.aspx?taxonid=292655&isprofile=1&basic=Symphyotrichum%20patens.

135. NCE Gardener Plant Toolbox, *"Symphyotrichum patens"* [clasping aster], https://plants.ces.ncsu.edu/plants/symphyotrichum-patens.

136. USDA NRCS Plants database, *"Symphyotrichum patens* (Aiton) G.L. Nesom, late purple aster," https://plants.usda.gov/home/plantProfile?symbol=SYPA11.

137. Prairie Moon Nursery, *"Liatris pycnostachya,* Prairie Blazing Star," https://www.prairiemoon.com/liatris-pycnostachya-prairie-blazing-star-prairie-moon-nursery.html; Illinois Wildflowers, "Prairie Blazingstar, *Liatris pycnostachya,"* illinoiswildflowers.info/prairie/plantx/pr_blazingstarx.htm.

138. Amy Stone, "Perennial of the Week—Liatris," Buckeye Yard & Garden onLine, The Ohio State University, July 4, 2017, bygl.osu.edu/node/808.

139. USDA NRCS Plants database, *"Liatris pycnostachya* Michx., prairie blazing star," https://plants.usda.gov/home/plantProfile?symbol=LIPY.

140. Prairie Moon Nursery, *"Liatris pycnostachya."*

141. Illinois Wildflowers, "Prairie Blazingstar."

142. USDA NRCS Plants database, *"Liatris aspera* Michx., tall blazing star," https://plants.usda.gov/home/plantProfile?symbol=LIAS.

143. USDA NRCS Plants database, *"Liatris elegans* (Walter) Michx., pinkscale blazing star," https://plants.usda.gov/home/plantProfile?symbol=LIEL.

144. USDA NRCS Plants database, *"Conoclinium coelestinum* (L.) DC., blue mistflower," https://plants.usda.gov/home/plantProfile?symbol=COCO13.

145. Illinois Wildflowers, "Mistflower, *Conoclinium coelestinum,"* illinoiswildflowers.info/wetland/plants/mistflower.htm.

146. MoBG, Plant Finder, *"Conoclinium coelestinum* 'Cori,'" http://www.missouribotanical garden.org/PlantFinder/PlantFinderDetails.aspx?taxonid=244424&isprofile=0&kempercode=f510%27.

147. USDA NRCS Plants database, *"Symphyotrichum dumosum* (L.) G.L. Nesom var. dumosum, rice button aster," https://plants.usda.gov/home/plantProfile?symbol=SYDUD2.

148. Illinois Wildflowers, "Rice Button Aster, *Symphyotrichum dumosum,"* illinoiswildflowers.info/savanna/plants/rb_aster.htm.

149. Illinois Wildflowers, "White Snakeroot, *Ageratina altissima,"* illinoiswildflowers.info/woodland/plants/wh_snakeroot.htm.

150. The Ohio State University, "White Snakeroot (*Ageratina altissima*)," *Ohio Perennial and Biennial Weed Guide,* https://weedguide.cfaes.osu.edu/singlerecord.asp?id=91.

151. John W. Allen, *It Happened in Southern Illinois* (Carbondale: Southern Illinois University Press, 1968), 5–6.

152. USDA NRCS Plants database, *"Ageratina altissima* (L.) R.M. King & H. Rob. var. *altissima,* white snakeroot," https://plants.usda.gov/home/plantProfile?symbol=AGALA.

153. G. L Nesom, *"Symphyotrichum pilosum* (Willdenow)," *Phytologia* 77 (1995): 289. Reprinted in *Flora of North America* 20," efloras.org/florataxon.aspx?flora_id=1&taxon_id=250067670.

154. Illinois Wildflowers, "Frost Aster, *Symphyotrichum pilosum*," illinoiswildflowers.info /weeds/plants/fr_aster.htm.

155. NCE Gardener Plant Toolbox, "*Helianthus angustifolius*" [narrowleaf sunflower], https://plants.ces.ncsu.edu/plants/helianthus-angustifolius.

156. USDA NRCS Plants database, "*Helianthus angustifolius* L., swamp sunflower," https:// plants.usda.gov/home/plantProfile?symbol=HEAN2.

157. MoBG, Plant Finder, "*Helianthus divaricatus*," https://www.missouribotanicalgarden .org/PlantFinder/PlantFinderComments.aspx?kempercode=k390.

158. Illinois Wildflowers, "Woodland Sunflower, *Helianthus divaricatus*," illinoiswildflowers .info/savanna/plants/wd_sunflower.html.

159. USDA NRCS Plants database, "*Helianthus divaricatus* L., woodland sunflower," https:// plants.usda.gov/home/plantProfile?symbol=HEDI2.

160. USDA NRCS Plants database, "*Chrysopsis pilosa* Nutt., soft goldenaster," https://plants .usda.gov/home/plantProfile?symbol=CHPI8.

161. USDA NRCS Plants database, "*Erigeron pulchellus* Michx. robin's plantain," https:// plants.usda.gov/home/plantProfile?symbol=ERPU.

162. Illinois Wildflowers, "Robin's Plantain, *Erigeron pulchellus*," illinoiswildflowers.info /savanna/plants/robin_plantain.htm.

163. NCE Gardener Plant Toolbox, "*Antennaria plantaginifolia*" [pussytoes], https://plants .ces.ncsu.edu/plants/antennaria-plantaginifolia.

164. Illinois Wildflowers, "Plantain-Leaved Pussytoes, *Antennaria plantaginifolia*," illinois wildflowers.info/savanna/plants/pl_pussytoes.htm.

165. LBJ Wildflower Center, Plant Database, "*Antennaria plantaginifolia*," https://www .wildflower.org/plants/result.php?id_plant=ANPL.

166. USDA NRCS Plants database, "*Vernonia texana* (A. Gray) Small, Texas ironweed," https://plants.usda.gov/home/plantProfile?symbol=VETE3.

167. LBJ Wildflower Center, Plant Database, "*Vernonia texana*," https://www.wildflower .org/plants/result.php?id_plant=VETE3.

168. NCE Gardener Plant Toolbox, "*Bidens aristosa*" [beggarticks], https://plants.ces.ncsu .edu/plants/bidens-aristosa.

169. USDA NRCS Plants database, "*Bidens aristosa* (Michx.) Britton, bearded beggarticks," https://plants.usda.gov/home/plantProfile?symbol=BIAR.

170. USDA NRCS Plants database, "*Elephantopus carolinianus* Raeusch., Carolina elephants foot," https://plants.usda.gov/home/plantProfile?symbol=ELCA3.

171. NCE Gardener Plant Toolbox, "*Elephantopus tomentosus*" [common elephant's foot], https://plants.ces.ncsu.edu/plants/elephantopus-tomentosu. Previously known as *Elephantopus carolinianus var. simplex* and *Elephantopus nudicaulis*.

172. Coastal Plain Plants wiki, "*Elephantopus tomentosus*," coastalplainplants.org/wiki/index .php/Elephantopus_tomentosus.

173. North Carolina Native Plant Society, "*Elephantopus tomentosus*, Common Elephant's-foot, etal.," plants.ncwildflower.org/plant_galleries/details/elephantopus-tomentosus.

174. Chris Reid, botanist, Louisiana State University, pers. comm.; USDA NRCS Plants database, "*Pseudognaphalium obtusifolium* (L.) Hilliard & B.L. Burtt, rabbit-tobacco," https://plants.usda.gov/home/plantProfile?symbol=PSOB3.

175. Illinois Wildflowers, "Sweet Everlasting, *Pseudognaphalium obtusifolium,*" illinoiswild flowers.info/prairie/plantx/sw_everlasting.htm.

176. LBJ Wildflower Center, Plant Database, "*Pseudognaphalium obtusifolium,*" https://www.wildflower.org/plants/result.php?id_plant=PSOB3; Jim P. Brock and Kenn Kaufman, *Kaufman Field Guide to Butterflies of North America* (New York: Hillstar Editions, 2003).

177. Larry Allain, USGS, "*Gaillardia aestivalis,* lanceleaf blanketflower, winkler gaillardia, prairie gaillardia," Plants of Louisiana, https://warcapps.usgs.gov/PlantID/Species/Details /3810; FNPS, "*Gaillardia aestivalis,*" https://www.fnps.org/plant/gaillardia-aestivalis.

178. NatureServe Explorer, "*Gaillardia aestivalis,* Lanceleaf Blanket-flower," https://explorer .natureserve.org/Taxon/ELEMENT_GLOBAL.2.158838/Gaillardia_aestivalis.

179. Flora of North America, "*Cirsium horridulum,*" http://floranorthamerica.org/Cirsium _horridulum.

180. NCE Gardener Plant Toolbox, "*Cirsium horridulum*" [bull thistle], https://plants.ces .ncsu.edu/plants/cirsium-horridulum; LBJ Wildflower Center, Plant Database, "*Cirsium horridulum,*" https://www.wildflower.org/plants/result.php?id_plant=CIHO2.

181. iNaturalist, "Bristle Thistle, *Cirsium horridulum,*" https://www.inaturalist.org/taxa /127269-Cirsium-horridulum.

182. Peggy Cornett, "*Solidago speciosa*—Showy Goldenrod," *Thomas Jefferson Encyclopedia,* https://www.monticello.org/site/research-and-collections/solidago-speciosa-showy -goldenrod.

183. Donna L. Long, "Attracting Pollinators with the Goldenrods," https://donnallong.com /attracting-pollinators-with-the-goldenrods.

184. Illinois Wildflowers, "Giant Goldenrod, *Solidago gigantea,*" illinoiswildflowers.info /wetland/plants/gt_goldenrod.htm.

185. USDA NRCS Plants database, "*Solidago odora* Aiton, anisescented," https://plants .usda.gov/home/plantProfile?symbol=SOOD; iNaturalist, "Sweet Goldenrod, *Solidago odora,*" inaturalist.org/taxa/131183-Solidago-odora.

186. USDA NRCS Plants database, "*Solidago ludoviciana* (A. Gray) Small, Louisiana goldenrod," https://plants.usda.gov/home/plantProfile?symbol=SOLU.

187. USDA NRCS Plants database, "*Solidago radula* Nutt., western rough goldenrod," https://plants.usda.gov/home/plantProfile?symbol=SORA.

188. USDA NRCS Plants database, "*Solidago petiolaris* Aiton, downy ragged goldenrod," https://plants.usda.gov/home/plantProfile?symbol=SOPE; NCE Gardener Plant Toolbox, "*Solidago petiolaris*" [downy ragged goldenrod], https://plants.ces.ncsu.edu/plants/solidago -petiolaris.

189. Illinois Wildflowers, "Downy Ragged Goldenrod, *Solidago petiolaris,*" illinoiswild flowers.info/savanna/plants/dr_goldenrod.html.

190. USDA NRCS Plants database, "*Solidago rugosa* Mill., wrinkleleaf goldenrod," https://plants.usda.gov/home/plantProfile?symbol=SORU2.

191. Illinois Wildflowers, "Wrinkle-Leaved Goldenrod, *Solidago rugosa,*" illinoiswild
flowers.info/savanna/plants/wl_goldenrod.htm.

192. Larry Allain, USGS, "*Solidago nitida,* shiny golden-rod," Plants of Louisiana, https://war
capps.usgs.gov/PlantID/Species/Details/3078; Plant Lust, "*Solidago nitida,*" https://plantlust
.com/plants/50644/solidago-nitida.

LITTLE PLANT DIVERSITY "HOT SPOTS"

1. I am not restoring 100 percent of the upland historic shortleaf pine-oak-hickory woodland on the Wafer Creek Ranch conservation easement. A significant amount of acreage remains
that could be taken into the restoration project in the future.

THE PROTECTION AND RESTORATION OF
WAFER CREEK RANCH

1. Latimore Smith, *A Forest Restoration Management Plan for Wafer Creek Ranch,* Lincoln
Parish, Louisiana, Nature Conservancy, Louisiana Field Office, March 2006.

ACTIONS ON WAFER CREEK RANCH TO REESTABLISH
THE NATIVE ECOSYSTEM

1. Presently, there is no requirement of pesticide certification for herbicide application on
one's private land.

2. Ron Panzer, "Compatibility of Prescribed Burning with the Conservation of Insects in
Small, Isolated Prairie Reserves," *Conservation Biology* 16, no. 5 (October 2002).

3. Andrew J. Beattie, *The Evolutionary Ecology of Ant–Plant Mutualisms* (Cambridge: Cambridge University Press, 1985).

4. Kim L. Coffey and L. Katherine Kirkman, "Seed Germination Strategies of Species with
Restoration Potential in a Fire-Maintained Pine Savanna," *Natural Areas Journal* 26, no. 3 (July 1,
2006): 289–299.

5. Jacqueline P. Ott, Jitka Klimešová, and David C Hartnett, "The Ecology and Significance
of Below-ground Bud Banks in Plants," *Annals of Botany* 123, no. 7 (June 2019): 1099–1118.

RESULTS SO FAR ON WAFER CREEK RANCH

1. David Breithaup and Chris Doffit, "Louisiana's 2020 Private Lands Conservation Champions," *Louisiana Wildlife Insider,* Spring/Summer 2021, https://www.wlf.louisiana.gov/assets
/Resources/Publications/Wildlife_Insider/2021_Spring_Summer_Wildlife_Insider.pdf;
"LDWF Press Outreach on Private Landowner Champions," *Lower Mississippi Valley Joint Venture,* https://us13.campaign-archive.com/?u=59b2e55b69c6f7af019e0ea4c&id=ebfdd7e4a6.

2. *Birds of Conservation Concern 2021: Migratory Bird Program,* US Fish and Wildlife
Service, 2021, https://www.fws.gov/sites/default/files/documents/birds-of-conservation
-concern-2021.pdf. Several specimens were netted and banded by Louisiana Tech ornithologist
Terri Maness and students.

3. C. C. Richmond, "David Daigle: Keeper of the Savanna," *Louisiana Wildlife Insider,* Fall/Winter 2020, https://www.wlf.louisiana.gov/assets/Resources/Publications/Wildlife _Insider/2020_Fall_Winter_Wildlife_Insider.pdf; George Lowery Jr., *The Mammals of Louisiana and its Adjacent Waters* (Baton Rouge: Louisiana State University Press, 1981).

Index

wild lettuce, 103
woolly croton. *See* goatweed
woolly ragwort, 99–100
wrinkleleaf goldenrod, 119–20 (Fig.
   153), 152
Yankee weed, 104
fracking, 128
Frangula caroliniana, 40
fungi, 8, 11, 34, 45, 47, 97, 122

Gaillardia aestivalis, 116
Galactia volubi, 77
Garlon 4, 135
Gentian, 87
Gentianaceae, 87
global warming. *See* climate change
Grand Isle Preserve, 167
grapefruit, 84
grass. *See* Poaceae
grasses
   arrowfeather threeawn, 45
   Bentawn plumegrass, 54–55
   big bluestem, 42–43, 52
   bird-beaked panicum, 56
   blazing stars, 43
   broomsedge, 45, 58, 156
   bushy bluestem, 59
   bushy broomsedge. *See* bushy
    bluestem
   Elliott's bluestem, 53, 139–40, 156
   false dandelion, 45
   flag grass. *See* rough dropseed
   goatweed, 45
   groundcherry, 90
   Gulf Coast (pink) muhlygrass, 56
   hidden dropseed. *See* rough dropseed
   lacegrass, 54
   little bluestem, 42–43, 44, 46–50, 52,
    121 (Fig. 153), 122 (Fig. 154), 139–40,
    147–48, 150, 156, 160
   longleaf woodoats, 59
   narrow plumegrass, 55

prairie threeawn grass, 58
purple coneflowers, 43
purple lovegrass, 54, 151
purpletop grass, 57
rough dropseed, 51, 161
silver plumegrass, 55
slender Indiangrass, 53, 121 (Fig. 153),
   155, 164
slender lespedeza, 73
slender woodoats, 59
splitbeard bluestem, 50, 139–40, 153
switchgrass, 42–43, 52
velvet panicgrass, 59–60
yellow Indiangrass, 42–43, 52–53
Grau, Peggy, 123
Great Plains, 42
Greenpeace, 7
greenhouse gas emissions, 20, 23–24, 46
Gulf of Mexico, 10, 43

habitat loss, 5–6, 13, 17–18, 26
Half-Earth, 9
hawthorns, 40
heath, 97–98
Helianthus angustifolius, 110–11
Helianthus divaricatus, 111
herbicide, 23, 104, 134–37, 147–48
Heterotheca subaxillaris, 102, 163
*Hidden Grasslands of the South: Natural
   History and Conservation,* 42–43
Highway Beautification Act of 1965, 123
Horton, J. W., 127
huckleberry, 40, 97
Hunt, Logan, 128
Hypericaceae, 84
Hypericum hypericoides, 84
Hypericum mutilum, 84

Ilex opaca, 131
Indian Pipe, 61, 97–98
indicator species, 45
Indonesia, 7